Increase Diversity in Your School Library Collection and Program

Written by

Michelle Easley, Ed.S.

PublisherCataloging-in-Publication Data
Names: Easley, Michelle, author.
Title: Increase diversity in your school library collection and program/Michelle Easley.
Description: First edition. | Atlanta, GA: Positive Push Press, 2017.| Includes index.
Identifiers: LCCN 2017912831 | ISBN 978-0-9798358-6-5
Subjects: LCSH: School Libraries | Multicultural Education
Classification: LCC Z675 | DDC 020

Positive Push Press, LLC
P. O. Box 43811
Atlanta, Georgia 30336
www.positivepushpress.com
ISBN: 978-0-9798358-6-5

Table of Contents

Diversity Defined

We owe it to our students to shatter the single story. By providing diverse collections and library programming, we add different perspectives and thus offer a more complete and balanced view of the world, history, cultures, and people. Libraries should contain books that serve as windows and mirrors. Books should act as windows for children, and adults for that matter, who can gaze through to learn more about a world with which they may be unfamiliar. Books should be mirrors for all to see a reflection of the world they live in, regardless of their background. "When children cannot find themselves reflected in the books they read, or when the images they see are distorted, negative, or laughable, they learn a powerful lesson about how they are devalued in the society of which they are a part."[1]

School library programs should be a mechanism by which the single story is shattered. Multiple points of views, varying ideas, and assorted philosophies on issues should be presented. When children read, they should either see a reflection of themselves in the material they are reading, or else experience other cultures and a look into the life of someone different than them. "The single story creates stereotypes, and the problem with stereotypes is not that they are untrue, but that they are incomplete. They make one story become the only story." [2]

The foundation of a diverse school library program is a diverse school library collection. A diverse collection should contain many genres, including fiction, non-fiction, biographies, and reference materials, but it should also offer students easy access to primary source documents. In many instances primary source documents help to shatter single stories by presenting alternative points of view. Furthermore, the diverse school library collection should be rich with print books, electronic books, audio books, primary source documents, multimedia objects, and other digital resources.

---

[1] Bishop, R.S. 1990. Walk tall in the world: African American literature for today's children. *The Journal of Negro Education*, 59(4), 556–565.

[2] Adichie, C.N. 2009. The danger of a single story [Video speech]. Retrieved from http://www.ted.com/talks/chimamanda_adichie_the_danger_of_a_single_story.html

Diverse school library programs may reduce bias and promote understanding among different groups of people, which decreases fear and increases peace and harmony. These types of programs empower students to take social change into their own hands and serve as true creators and change agents by providing opportunities for students to enhance their critical thinking and analytical skills. Ultimately, this prepares students to live and work successfully in our global society. "By including diversity in its programs and collections, the library has the potential for helping children make cross-cultural connections and develop the skills necessary to function in a culturally pluralistic society."[3]

What does diversity really mean? It is much more than race and ethnicity. Diversity also includes socioeconomic class, gender, age, sexual orientation, mental or physical ability, religion, national geographic origin, language, and veteran status. It also includes family composition—such as adoption, same-gender parental units, single-parent families, extended parenting units, and other "non-conventional" family units—as well as living situation, such as homelessness, those living in poverty, and incarceration.[4]

An additional impetus for creating diverse library programs is the guidance set forth in the principles of the American Library Association's *Library Bill of Rights*, which apply equally to all libraries, including school libraries. Under these principles, all students have equitable access to library facilities, resources, and instructional programs.

I. Books and other library resources should be provided for the interest, information, and enlightenment of all people of the community the library serves. Materials should not be excluded because of the origin, background, or views of those contributing to their creation.

II. Libraries should provide materials and information presenting all points of view on current and historical issues. Materials should not be proscribed or removed because of partisan or doctrinal disapproval.

III. Libraries should challenge censorship in the fulfillment of their responsibility to provide information and enlightenment.

IV. Libraries should cooperate with all persons and groups concerned with resisting abridgment of free expression and free access to ideas.

---

[3] Naidoo, J. 2014. The importance of diversity in library programs and material collections for children. Written for the Association for Library Service to Children.

[4] iUniversity of California-Berkeley Center for Equity, Inclusion and Diversity. (n.d.). "Glossary of terms." http://diversity.berkeley.edu/glossary-terms (accessed on December 2, 2016).

V. A person's right to use a library should not be denied or abridged because of origin, age, background, or views.[5]

Furthermore, the ALA Code of Ethics states, "We provide the highest level of service to all library users through appropriate and usefully organized resources; equitable service policies; equitable access; and accurate, unbiased, and courteous responses to all requests."[6]

The Code of Ethics should serve as a foundation by which school library programs are designed and should guide the school librarian's work. Number 1 speaks to the inclusion of diverse materials and programming that meets the needs of all users. Diversity is one of the core values of the American Association of Librarians.[7]

Are You Aware?

Dack and Tomlinson (2015) offer four steps that will help others be more aware of different cultures to help all students succeed.[8]

1. Recognize and appreciate cultural variance.
2. Learn about and look for culturally influenced learning patterns.
3. Look beyond cultural patterns to see individuals.
4. Plan inviting curriculum and instruction.

---

[5] American Library Association. 1996. "Library Bill of Rights." <http://www.ala.org/advocacy/intfreedom/librarybill> (accessed December 2, 2016).

[6] American Library Association. 2008. "Code of Ethics of the American Library Association." <http://www.ala.org/advocacy/proethics/codeofethics/codeethics> (accessed December 2, 2016).

[7] American Library Association. "Equity, Diversity and Inclusion".<http://www.ala.org/advocacy/diversity> (accessed January 2, 2016).

[8] Dack, H., & Tomlinson, C. A. 2015. Inviting All Students to Learn. *Educational Leadership*, 72(6), 10-15.

These four steps can benefit school librarians when designing programming. Making room for differences in the library program presents differentiated learning opportunities and allows students to see themselves as individuals. Programming that respects and values the differences between students fosters a collaborative environment, which ultimately leads to a positive school library climate. You will know your program is a success when every student, regardless of differences, feels welcomed and valued.

"If you talk to a man in a language he understands, that goes to his head. If you talk to him in his language, that goes to his heart".
—*Nelson Mandela*

Collection Evaluation

How can you evaluate your own collection to determine if it is diverse? Unfortunately, you can't just hit a "Is my collection diverse?" button—but you can make an assessment. There are a few different approaches, each of which require you to dissect your collection. First, you can use the list of titles found in this book or in other sources to check and see how many diverse titles you have in your collection. In essence, run a title list to determine if your library's catalog contains diverse titles.

Another approach is to select one section of your library—say, the Easy section, letter A. Physically go through all of the titles in the letter A, pulling each book one by one, scanning them to determine if they reflect visual representations of diversity with their pictures, words, or text. This is undoubtedly easier to do for pictures books than say, young adult novels. As such, this method may be time-consuming.

A third approach is completing a keyword search and recording your findings for each of the keywords listed in the chart that appears in this section. Note how many titles appear in the results when you do a search for the keywords listed, further noting the section the titles appear in, i.e., fiction, nonfiction, biography, etc.

Review your results by answering the following questions:
a. Does your collection represent diverse world views?
b. Do you have titles related to diverse subjects in all sections, such as fiction and non-fiction?
c. Do you have people from various ethnic and cultural backgrounds represented in your biography section?
d. Do you have titles in diverse formats: hardcover, paperback, electronic, audio, etc.?
e. If you are in a K – 5 environment, is diversity represented in your easy, juvenile, and young adult fiction sections?

Remember, many nonfiction and fiction titles that represent diverse authors or topics may not be returned in this keyword search. You may need to print some of the suggested lists included in this book and search your collection for these titles or authors.

Analyzing Your Collection For Diverse Titles

Keyword	# Of Titles	Nonfiction	Fiction	Biography	Other
African					
African American					
American Indian					
Asian					
Black					
Chinese					
Chinese American					
Disability					
Disabled					
Gay					
Hispanic					
Homeless					
Homelessness					
Homosexual					
Immigrant					
Japanese					
Japanese American					
Korean					
Latino					
Lesbian					
Native American					
Poverty					
Transgender					

*This list is not intended to be all-inclusive but should serve as a starting point

Additional Questions to ask:

- Does the book have a main character from a diverse background?
- Is it set in a country other than the United States?
- Is it set in an immigrant community within the United States?

- Does it involve experiences outside of middle class America? Homelessness? Poverty?
- Are the characters of diverse religious faiths?
- Does it include topics of diverse religious faiths?
- Does it include topics of interest to both genders?
- Does it include words or phrases in a language other than English?

It is a great idea to solicit the support of your book distributor when increasing your collection's diversity, as they can often offer assistance. Many distributors provide collection analysis via an online collection analysis tool. Generally, the school librarian uploads MARC records to the vendor's website, and the vendor provides an analysis. This analysis allows you to easily see the age of your collection, a breakdown by Dewey category, and its strengths and weaknesses. Online collection analysis may assist you in determining how diverse your collection is and provide you with information to grow a more diverse collection. In doing research for this book, I contacted several vendors for more information on how they assist with evaluating the diversity of a collection. This information appears in the next few paragraphs; however, it should not be considered as an endorsement of any particular vendor, but rather as a presentation of information.

Veronica Evans of Leading LLC takes on the role of a consultant for school librarians. In addition to researching the demographics of a school community, her company has instituted the following methods to meet the needs of diversity within a school:

1. Acquire information from MDR (Market Data Retrieval).
2. Provide wish lists and surveys to faculty and staff for requesting diverse titles.
3. Meet one-on-one with decision-makers and solicit responses for needed areas of diversity.
4. Offer book collaboration workshops to allow for discussion among stakeholders on books needed to yield the best results within their building.
5. Attend conferences and read literature to stay aware of diversity needs so the company may be an asset in presenting diverse literature to its customers.
6. Work with authors and publishing companies to publish books that meet the needs of a diverse population.

Veronica works with her clients to drill down to the Dewey numbers that cover specific categories of diversity, but she has found the most useful method has been one that requires her to converse directly with clients and stakeholders. Additionally, she works to get an understanding of the needs of the students of her clients. These discussions have made their way to the publishers. Veronica shares that she has had the opportunity to witness the difference these conversations have made in the types of books published over the years. She comments that publishing companies have listened to the need for diversity. It is a win, win, win! leadingllc.mybooksandmore.com

Follett School Solutions offers collection analysis through Title wise, a collection analysis tool that allows librarians to identify strengths and weaknesses of their collection. The tool generates a collection analysis report that includes summaries by Dewey numbers, balanced Dewey comparisons, collection by year, age sensitivity, aged titles, and more.

Seth Gumble, Director of IT at Follett School Solutions, states that Follett's Title wise Collection Analysis tool can be helpful for school librarians as they evaluate diversity in their library collection. Follett is also developing a discovery tool that can help school librarians assess their collection by using MARC records, BISAC categories, Follett's curriculum tags, and other metadata, including Follett-assigned subjects or topics that relate to diversity. This tool would be valuable to school librarians, enabling them to use an automated process to generate a starting point in the analysis process. https://www.titlewave.com/

Policy Analysis

"An individual has not started living until he can rise above the narrow confines of his individualistic concerns to the broader concerns of all humanity."

Martin Luther King, Jr.

The goal of library policy should be to provide access to all students. In The AASL Position Statement on the Role of the School Librarian in Reading, the American Association of School Librarians stated that school libraries must provide "open, non-restricted access to a varied high quality collection of reading materials in multiple formats that reflect academic needs and personal interests."[1]

Circulation of Material

What is your circulation policy? When is the last time you reflected on your policy and how it might impact various groups of students in your school? Most policies are in place for valid reasons. For example, many school libraries don't loan reference material due to the high price point per item. Does your school have a policy of not loaning reference materials?

Some students lack access to the Internet, so seemingly simple homework assignments become difficult. In some instances, allowing a student to take a particular volume of the encyclopedia home may make a tremendous difference. It may be helpful to allow students to take home reference books and return them overnight or after some other specified period of time.

How many books can students check out at a time? Can they check out an additional book if they return a book late?

In some schools, Kindergarten or pre-Kindergarten children can check out a limited number of books, such as one book at a time. Some of these very same students may be from homes where print resources are limited due to socioeconomic status. Therefore, it may be worth considering allowing Kindergarten and pre-Kindergarten students to borrow more than one book at a time. If family members are willing to read to the children, having multiple titles on hand would be beneficial.

Fines Policies

What is your fines policy? Do you charge a set amount per day or per type of item? Do you cap the amount at some maximum? Now consider your population. Do you work in a school where many students receive free or reduced lunch? Do you work with homeless students? Could your fine policy be impacting who actually fully engages with your library program? Instead of charging fines per day, could you allow students to volunteer hours when returning overdue books or some other creative form or repayment? If a student loses a book, could you use donations from the PTA or other organizations to pay for the student's lost books? It is disheartening that some students may not check out books to take home because they know if they misplace the book, they won't be able to afford to pay to replace it.

School Library Hours of Operation

What are your hours of operation? Do they make it easier or harder for students and families to access the school library? If you serve students that ride the school bus, they may be limited in the time they have to visit the library before or after school. If it is difficult for them to leave class and visit the library, are your hours supporting their use of the library? Have you reflected on how parents in your community are able to visit your library? Are they welcome to visit, volunteer, or use your resources to help their children? Many parents whose native language is not English may find the school and its library intimidating. Do you go the extra step to lessen this feeling for them?

Consider extending your hours one day per week to allow parents to visit with their children. You could open an hour earlier or stay open an hour later in the evening. Present this idea to your administration; this may be able to be accomplished through flexible scheduling of your work hours or utilizing volunteers.

Have you ever considered holding Saturday hours once per month? This may allow you to reach parents and students who might otherwise never engage with your library program. Again, seek out the support of your administration to make this work.

POLICY REFLECTION

DATE:

Circulation of Material

How many items can each student check out?

Grade level	# of items

Can students check out reference materials?

Fines

What are your fines for overdue material?

What is the fine or fee for lost material?

Hours of Operation

What are your hours of operation?

Could you extend or revise your schedule to allow for different parent and student access?

Select one policy from above and indicate how it could be changed to benefit DIVERSE student needs?

Once you have evaluated your collection and determined where you stand, you should set goals for growing your collection. You will find a SMART goal template at the end of this book. SMART goals are goals that are specific, measurable, attainable, relevant, and time-bound. These goals can be used as a part of your overall plan for your school library media program. [9]

> *"We all should know that diversity makes for a rich tapestry, and we must understand that all the threads of the tapestry are equal in value no matter what their color."*
> —*Maya Angelou*

---

[9] American Association of School Librarians. (2010). "Position Statement on the School Librarian's Role in Reading." <http://www.ala.org/aasl/advocacy/resources/statements/reading-role> (accessed on December 9, 2016).

Diverse Collection Classification

Once you have acquired diverse titles, consideration should be given to the physical space that houses these titles. A diverse library collection deserves a space to support it.

To Dewey or not to Dewey, that is the question. As Librarians, we classify knowledge, and in many school libraries this classification is based on Dewey, first introduced in 1876. However, we rarely take the time to reflect on how Eurocentric the Dewey Classification system really is. The Dewey Classification system may in fact make many topics that relate to diversity more difficult to find. Take a moment to look at the hundreds divisions on the next page. Does anything jump out at you?

The Library of Congress (LC) Subject Headings may create a similar situation. Established in 1898, the LC subject headings are controlled vocabulary used for indexing, cataloging, and searching for bibliographic records in library catalogs and electronic databases. This controlled vocabulary can reflect bias. Consider, for example, that call numbers related to homosexuality were under the rubric of Abnormal Sex Relations until the 1920s[10]. The Dewey Decimal System classified these types of books under Mental Illnesses until the 1930s. This has evolved to today, where homosexuality is classed in the 306s.

A student group and university librarians at Dartmouth College, Hanover, NH, in collaboration with the American Library Association, worked to have the term illegal alien removed from the Library of Congress (LC) Subject Headings. This occurred

---

[10] AUMANN, J. 2015. File Under Queer. *Publishers Weekly*, 262(21), 24-25.

not in 1950 but rather in 2016. The term was replaced with non-citizen to describe the act of residing without authorization, or unauthorized immigration. "Illegal aliens" will become a "former heading," cross-referenced with the new terminology; other headings that include the phrase will be revised or canceled.[11]

The question of whether or not to arrange your library by Dewey numbers or LC subject headings is personal or perhaps tied to a district mandate. There is no right or wrong answer. The most important thing to remember is that you should make resources easy for your students to find and respect differences.

The Hundred Divisions of the Dewey Decimal System

Reflect on the hundred divisions of the Dewey Decimal System?

What do you notice as it relates to classifying items related to diverse topics?

[11] Peet, L. 2016. LC Drops "Illegal Alien" Subject Heading. *Library Journal*, 141(11), 12-13.

Grow a Diverse Collection

One method of adding to your collection is to add award-winning titles. This is a great way to get started in growing a diverse collection. You can locate the award-winning titles from the award categories listed below. These awards feature titles that are diverse books. The award descriptions are what appear on each award's webpage. Many book distributors curate lists of these award-winning titles, making it very easy to purchase them.

Jane Addams Children's Book Award

http://www.janeaddamspeace.org/jacba/about.shtml

The Jane Addams Children's Book Award annually recognizes children's books of literary and aesthetic excellence that effectively engage children in thinking about peace, social justice, global community, and equity for all people. Jane Addams was a co-founder and the first President of the Women's International League for Peace and Freedom.

2016 Award for Younger Children

New Shoes by Susan Lynn Meyer

2016 Award for Older Children

Turning 15 on the Road to Freedom: My Story of the 1965 Selma Voting Rights March by Lynda Blackmon Lowery as told to Elspeth Leacock and Susan Buckley

American Indian Youth Literature Award

http://ailanet.org/activities/american-indian-youth-literature-award

The awards were established as a way to identify and honor the very best writing and illustrations by and about American Indians.

2016 Picture Book

Little You by Richard Van Camp

2016 Middle School

In the Footsteps of Crazy Horse by Joseph Marshall II

2016 Young Adult Winner

House of Purple Cedar by Tim Tingle

Americas Award

http://www.claspprograms.org/americasaward

Consortium of Latin American Studies Program founded the Américas Award in 1993 to encourage and commend authors, illustrators and publishers who produce quality children's and young adult books that portray Latin America, the Caribbean, or Latinos in the United States.

2016 Award Winners

Echo by Pam Muñoz Ryan
Out of Darkness by Ashley Hope-Pérez

Arab American Book Award

http://www.arabamericanmuseum.org/bookaward

The Arab American Book Awards is a literary program created to honor books written by and about Arab Americans.

2016 Award Winners

Fiction

A Curious Land: Stories of Home by Susan Muaddi Darraj

The Evelyn Shakir Non-Fiction Award

Handbook of Arab American Psychology edited by Mona M. Amer and Germine H. Award
This Muslim American Life: Dispatches from the War on Terror by MoustafaBayoumi

The George Ellenbogen Poetry Award

The Republics by Nathalie Handal

Honorable Mentions

Fiction

In the Language of Miracles by Rajia Hassib

Poetry

Sand Opera by Philip Metres

Asian/Pacific American Award for Literature

http://www.apalaweb.org/awards/literature-awards/

Honors and recognizes individual work about Asian/Pacific Americans and their heritage, based on literary and artistic merit.

2016 Winners
Young Adult

P.S. I Still Love You by Jenny Han

Children's

Full Cicada Moon by Marilyn Hilton

Picture Book

Juna's Jar by Jane Bahk

Mildred L. Batchelder Award

http://www.ala.org/alsc/awardsgrants/bookmedia/batchelderaward

    The Batchelder Award is given to the most outstanding children's book originally published in a language other than English in a country other than the United States, and subsequently translated into English for publication in the United States.

2016 Winner

Cry, Heart, But Never **Break by Glenn Ringtved**

Pura Belpre Awards

http://www.ala.org/alsc/awardsgrants/bookmedia/belpremedal

    The award is named after Pura Belpré, the first Latina librarian at the New York Public Library. The Pura Belpré Award, established in 1996, is presented annually to a Latino/Latina writer and illustrator whose work best portrays, affirms, and celebrates the Latino cultural experience in an outstanding work of literature for children and youth.

2017 Author Award

Juana & Lucas **written and illustrated by Juana Medina**

2017 Illustrator Award

Lowriders to the Center of the Earth **illustrated by Raúl Gonzalez, written by Cathy Camper**

Coretta Scott King Book Awards

http://www.ala.org/emiert/cskbookawards

Presented annually to outstanding African American authors and illustrators of books for children and young adults that demonstrate an appreciation of African American culture and universal human values.

2017 Book Award

March Book: Three by Congressman John Lewis and Andrew Aydin

2017 Illustrator Award

Radiant Child: The Story of Young Artist Jean-Michel Basquiat by Javaka Steptoe

In The Margins Book Award

http://www.youthlibraries.org/margins-book-award-selection-committee
This award is presented by a committee under the umbrella of Library Services for Youth in Custody. This organization serves the needs of and advocating for those who provide library services for youth in custody, which would include, incarcerated/detained/committed youth in both juvenile & adult settings in municipal, county, local, state, or federal facilities, including ICE detention centers and youth in secure mental health or rehab settings, and might also include at-risk youth in other forms of group housing or government custody.

2017 Top Fiction

Little Miss Somebody by Christy Lynn Abram

2017 Top Nonfiction

Aging Out by Alton Carter
2017 In The Margins Social Justice/Advocacy Award
Who Do You Serve, Who Do You Protect? by Maya Shenwar

The Social Justice/Advocacy Award recognizes books that focus on issues of race, class and incarceration or highlights what life is like for people living in the margins of society. This award is presented to adult books.

Tomas Rivera Mexican American Children's Book Award

http://www.education.txstate.edu/ci/riverabookaward/
This award honors authors and illustrators who create literature that depicts the Mexican American experience.

2016 Award Winner

Duncan Tonatiuh's Funny Bones: Posada and His Day of the Dead Calaveras by Jose Guadalupe Posada

Out of Darkness by Ashley Hope Pérez

Schneider Family Book Award

http://www.ala.org/awardsgrants/schneider-family-book-award

   This award honors an author or illustrator for a book that embodies an artistic expression of the disability experience for child and adolescent audiences.

Teen Book

When We Collided by Emery Lord

Middle School Book

As Brave As You by Jason Reynolds

Young Children's Book

Six Dots: A Story of Young Louis Braille by Jen Bryan

Skipping Stones Honor Awards

http://www.skippingstones.org/2016.BookAwards.pdf

   Award is granted to books that promote an understanding of culture, promote cooperation and an understanding of diversity.

Winners – Multicultural & International Books

Baby Talk Bilingual Board Books/Palabras del bebé Libros Bilingües by Katherine Del Monte

I am Hapa! by Crystal Smith

Lo que mi abuela me dijo/What My Grandmother Told Me: Practical Wisdom from Spanish Proverbs and Sayings by Maria Paz Eleizegui Weir

*El Día de losMuertos/The Remembering Day*written and illustrated by Pat Mora

My Tata's Remedies/Los remedios de mi tata by Roni Capin Rivera-Ashford

Lailah's Lunchbox: A Ramadan Story by Reem Faruqi

Mango, Abuela, and Me by Meg Medina

Growing up Pedro: How the Martinez Brothers Made It from the Dominican Republic All the Way to the Major Leagues by Matt Tavare

The Green Musician by Mahvash Shahegh

Pine and the Winter Sparrow Retold by Alexis York Lumbard

Whispers of the Wolf by Pauline Ts'o

Daddy's Heart, My Heart, The Purple Heart by Angela Kohout, Madeline Murillo, and Elizabeth Sagi

Voice of Freedom, Fannie Lou Hamer: Spirit of the Civil Rights Movement by Carole Boston Weatherford

For The Right to Learn: Malala Yousafzai's Story by Rebecca Langston-George

Child Soldier: When Boys and Girls Are Used in War by Jessica Dee Humphreys and Michel Chikwanine

Prison Boy by Sharon E. McKay

Stella by Starlight by Sharon M. Draper

Give Me Wings: How a Choir of Former Slaves Took on the World by Kathy Lowinger

My Seneca Village by Marilyn Nelson

The Hero Twins: A Navajo-English Story of the Monster Slayers by Jim Kristofic

Enchanted Air: Two Cultures, Two Wings by Margarita Engle

Urban Tribes: Native Americans in the City edited by Lisa Charleyboy and Mary Beth Leatherdale

Dolly Gray Children's Literature Award

http://daddcec.org/awards/dollygrayawards.aspx

   Award presented to authors, illustrators, and publishers of high quality fiction and biography children, intermediate, and young adult books that appropriately portray individuals with developmental disabilities.

2016 Award

My Friend Suhana by Shaila Abdullah and Aanyah Abdullah
Rain Reign by Ann M. Martin

Ezra Jack Keats Award

http://www.ezra-jack-keats.org/section/ezra-jack-keats-book-awards/
This award is presented to recognize and encourage new writers and new illustrators in the field of children's books. The award highlights works that portray universal qualities of childhood, a strong and supportive family and the multicultural nature of the world.

2016 New Writer Award

Poet: The Remarkable Story of George Moses Horton by Don Tate

2016 New Illustrator Award

Sonya's Chicken by Phoebe Wahl

Stonewall Book Awards

http://www.ala.org/glbtrt/award/stonewall/
Awarded to a notable Gay, Lesbian, Bisexual, and Transgender title.

2017 Barbara Gittings Literature Award

Desert Boys by Chris McCormick

Israel Fishman Nonfiction Award

How to Survive a Plague: The inside story of how citizens and science tamed AIDS by David France

Lambda Literary Award

http://www.lambdaliterary.org/awards/
The Lambda Literary Awards identify and celebrate the best lesbian, gay, bisexual and transgender books of the year and affirm that LGBTQ stories are part of the literature of the world.

LGBT Children's/Young Adult

George by Alex Gino

Mike Morgan & Larry Romans Children's & Young Adult Literature Award

Magnus Chase and the Gods of Asgard: The Hammer of Thor by Rick Riordan
If I Was Your Girl by Meredith Russo

Stonewall Honor Books in Children's and Young Adult Literature

When the Moon Was Ours by Anna-Marie McLemore
Unbecoming by Jenny Downham
Pride: Celebrating Diversity & Community by Robin Stevenson

Sydney Taylor Book Awards

http://jewishlibraries.org/content.php?page=Sydney_Taylor_Book_Award
    Presented by the Association of Jewish Libraries to outstanding books for children and teens that authentically portray the Jewish experience.

The Sydney Taylor Book Award Winner for Younger Readers

I Dissent: Ruth Bader Ginsburg Makes Her Mark by Debbie Levy with illustrations by Elizabeth Baddeley

The Sydney Taylor Book Award Winner for Older Readers

The Inquisitor's Tale: Or, The Three Magical Children and Their Holy Dog by Adam Gidwitz

The Sydney Taylor Book Award Winner for Teen Readers

Anna and the Swallow Man by Gavriel Savit

Carter G. Woodson Book Awards

http://www.socialstudies.org/awards/woodson
Presented to exemplary books written for children and young people.

Elementary Winner

Poet: The Remarkable Story of George Moses Horton by Don Tate
The Amazing Age of John Roy Lynch by Chris Barton

Secondary Winner

Passenger on the Pearl: The True Story of Emily Edmonson's Flight from Slavery by Winifred Conkling

Lists to Know

If you are looking for curated lists, you should also consider the lists below. These lists can be used to grow your collection and serve as an excellent starting point. Consider adding titles from these lists in print, electronic, or audio format.

Rainbow Book List

http://glbtrt.ala.org/rainbowbooks/archives/1255
    Bibliography of books with significant gay, lesbian, bisexual, transgender, or queer/questioning content, which are aimed at youth, birth through age 18.

Amelia Bloomer Book List

http://www.ala.org/awardsgrants/amelia-bloomer-book-list
    Bibliography of books with significant feminist content.

> *We inhabit a universe that is characterized by diversity.*
>
> *Desmond Tutu*

How Do I Find Diverse Books?

FOLLOW...

#WENEEDDIVERSE BOOKS

http://weneeddiversebooks.org/

We Need Diverse Books is a nonprofit organization supporting diversity in children's literature with special events, panel discussions, writing contests, grant awards, mentorships, and resources for teachers and librarians.

VISIT...

American Indians in Children's Literature

https://americanindiansinchildrensliterature.blogspot.com/
    Critical perspectives and analysis of indigenous peoples in children's and young adult books, the school curriculum, popular culture, and society.

The Brown Book Shelf

https://thebrownbookshelf.com/

Children's Book Council Diversity Reading Lists

http://www.cbcdiversity.com/resources/teachersandlibrarians

Color in Colorado!

http://www.colorincolorado.org/

Bilingualsite for educators and families of English language learners. Maintained by the American Federation of Teachers and the National Education Association.

Cooperative Children's Book Center – 30 Multicultural Books Every Teen Should Know

http://ccbc.education.wisc.edu/books/detailListBooks.asp?idBookLists=253

Cooperative Children's Book Center – 50 Multicultural Books Every Child Should Know

http://ccbc.education.wisc.edu/books/detailListBooks.asp?idBookLists=42

Disability in Kid Lit

http://disabilityinkidlit.wordpress.com/

Finding Wonderland

http://writingya.blogspot.com/

This blog highlights young adult books, especially speculative fiction, adventure, suspense, and graphic novels, with diverse characters (including diversity of body/ability, ethnicity, culture, gender, and faith).

I'm Queer. I'm Here. What the Hell do I Read?

http://www.leewind.org/

This blog highlights YA books with GLBTQ characters and themes, plus much more.

I'm Your Neighbor

http://www.imyourneighborbooks.org/
   Promotes the use of children's literature featuring "new arrival" cultures and groups. The site contains recommended list of books and projects for educators, librarians, and community organizations.

Latinos in Kid Lit

https://latinosinkidlit.com/
   Information about young adult, middle grade, and young adult Latinx literature.

Lee and Low Publishers Blog

http://blog.leeandlow.com/2017/01/23/announcing-our-2016-new-voices-award-winner/
   Excellent information about all things diverse literature.

Mitali Perkins (author)

http://www.mitaliblog.com/

Rich in Color

http://richincolor.com/
   Provides reviews of and promotes young adult books (fiction and non-fiction) starring or written by people of color or people from First/Native Nations.

Vamos A Leer: Teaching Latin America Through Literacy

https://teachinglatinamericathroughliterature.wordpress.com/
   Vamos a Leer is managed by the Latin American and Iberian Institute (LAII) at the University of New Mexico. The LAII is designated a National Resource Center for Latin America by the U.S. Department of Education. The *Vamos a Leer Blog* supports K-12 teaching about Latin America. Here you will find lesson plans as well as author and book suggestions.

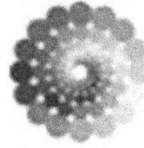

Perspectives for a Diverse America

http://perspectives.tolerance.org/

Perspectives for a Diverse America is a K-12 literacy-based, anti-bias online curriculum. The main component of Perspectives is the Central Text Anthology, a curated collection of 350 diverse texts including literature, multimedia, informational, and visual. The texts reflect diversity as it relates to ability, community, immigration, race, ethnicity, class, place, gender, LGBT, and religion. Perspectives include the anchor standards and domains of identity, diversity, justice, and action. This is a project of the Southern Poverty Law Center and Teaching Tolerance.

This anthology is perfect for the school librarian. It contains invaluable information that can be used when instructing students; working with staff members; or setting your program's goals, objectives, and activities. The curriculum can be worked through as a stand-alone program or used as a guide for structuring library activities.

Features Integrated Learning Plan

Grades K – 2

- Explore texts through read-alouds
- Students respond to the texts
- Do Something – students participate in activities that require civic engagement

Grades 3 – 12

- Word Work – students learn key vocabulary and use it as their own
- Close and Critical Reading – students analyze and build reading comprehension skills

- Write to the Source – respond to ideas in the central text through personal writing
- Do Something – students respond with action
- Community Inquiry – students use speaking and listening skills in response to the text and relate to the anti-bias standards

Printed with permission from Perspectives for a Diverse Americahttp://perspectives.tolerance.org/

Reading Diversity – Tool for Selecting Diverse Texts

Teaching Tolerance has also developed another impressive tool that will aid in selecting diverse texts, Reading Diversity. This tool uses four dimensions for text selection: complexity, diversity and representation, critical literacy and reader and task.[12]

Teaching Tolerance has two tools available:

- Extended Edition *http://www.tolerance.org/sites/default/files/general/ Reading%20Diversity--Extended%20Edition2016_VFF.pdf*
- Teacher Edition *http://www.tolerance.org/sites/default/files/general/ Reading%20Diversity%20Lite%E2%80%94Teacher%27s%20Edition2.pdf*

Either of these tools would be very useful when making text selections. Additionally, if you are working with teachers and other school staff it provides a beautiful framework for an in-depth discussion about diverse texts. If you are meeting with your media committee, friends of the library, parent groups, school leadership and/or community members this is an excellent vehicle to use to build understanding around quality diverse text selection. You could review the sample completed tool with a group during a meeting or professional learning session. http://www.tolerance.org/ sites/default/files/general/Hot%2C%20Hot%20Roti%20Lite%20Tool.pdf

---

[12] Teaching Tolerance (2015). "Reading Diversity: A Tool for Selecting Diverse Texts." <http://www.tolerance.org/sites/default/files/ general/Reading%20Diversity--Extended%20Edition2016_VFF.pdf> accessed December 4, 2016.

Around the World in a Year

January

January 16 – Martin Luther King Day

National holiday celebrating the life and legacy of Rev. Dr. Martin Luther King, Jr.
http://www.thekingcenter.org/making-king-holiday

January 28 – Chinese New Year

http://www.infoplease.com/spot/chinesenewyear1.html

February

African American History Month

http://www.africanamericanhistorymonth.gov/
https://www.loc.gov/law/help/commemorative-observations/african-american.php
http://constitutioncenter.org/learn/civic-calendar/african-american-history-month
http://www.pbs.org/black-culture/explore/10-black-history-little-known-facts/#.
WIF-TIMrLIU
http://www.loc.gov/teachers/classroommaterials/primarysourcesets/
harlem-renaissance/
Library of Congress Primary Source Documents – The Harlem Renaissance
http://www.loc.gov/teachers/classroommaterials/primarysourcesets/naacp/
Library of Congress Primary Source – The NAACP

March

National Women's History Month

http://www.loc.gov/teachers/classroommaterials/primarysourcesets/
womens-suffrage/

Library of Congress Primary Source Documents – Women's Suffrage
http://womenshistorymonth.gov/
http://www.loc.gov/teachers/classroommaterials/themes/womens-history/
https://www.nps.gov/wori/learn/education/index.htm
http://www.nwhp.org/
http://teacher.scholastic.com/activities/women/index.htm
http://www.nea.org/tools/lessons/50850.htm
Women's History Month Lesson Ideas K – 12

March 1 – Zero Discrimination Day

An annual worldwide event that promotes diversity and recognizes that everyone counts. The United Nations program on Human Immunodeficiency Virus (HIV) and Acquired Immune Deficiency Syndrome (AIDS), launched its Zero Discrimination Campaign on World AIDS Day in December 2013.
http://www.unaids.org/en/resources/campaigns/2016_zerodiscriminationday

March 2 – Read Across America Day

Celebrate the birthday of Dr. Seuss with a reading awareness and motivation celebration.
http://www.readacrossamerica.org/
Read Across America Pledge

March 5 – 11 – Teen Tech Week

March 8 – International Women's Day

International Women's Day (March 8) is a global day celebrating the social, economic, cultural, and political achievements of women.
https://www.internationalwomensday.com
http://www.un.org/en/events/womensday/
United Nations International Women's Day

March 16 – Freedom of Information Day

http://www.ala.org/advocacy/advleg/federallegislation/govinfo/opengov/freedomofinfo
The birthday of President James Madison, "Father of the Constitution" and known as the foremost advocate for openness in government.

March 17 – St. Patrick's Day

What started as a religious feast day for the patron saint of Ireland now has become an international festival celebrating Irish culture.

March 31 – Ceasar Chavez Day

Celebrate the life and legacy of the civil rights and labor movement activist Cesear Chavez.
https://obamawhitehouse.archives.gov/the-press-office/2016/03/30/presidential-proclamation-cesar-chavez-day-2016
Presidential Proclamation for Cesear Chavez Day

April

School Library Month

National Poetry Month

http://www.loc.gov/teachers/classroommaterials/primarysourcesets/poetry/
Library of Congress Primary Source documents – Found Poetry Collection

April 2 – Autism Day

April 7 – World Health Day

April 12 – D.E.A.R. Drop Everything and Read

April 9 – 15 – National Library Week

April 16 – Easter

April 22 – Earth Day

April 23 – National Readathon Day

http://www.readathonday.com/

April 30 – International Jazz Day

April 30 – Children's Book Day/El día de los niños/El día de los libros

May

Childrens Book Week

Asian Pacific American Heritage Month
http://asianpacificheritage.gov/
http://apasf.org/
http://asianpacificheritage.gov/

May 5 – Cinco De Mayo

https://www.britannica.com/topic/Cinco-de-Mayo

May 27 – Ramadan Starts

http://www.history.com/topics/holidays/ramadan

June

Gay Lesbian Pride Month
https://www.loc.gov/lgbt/about.html

GLBT Book Month

Celebration of the authors and writings that reflect the lives and experiences of the gay, lesbian, bisexual, and transgender community. This is an initiative of the American Library Association
http://www.ala.org/glbtrt/glbt-book-month

June 19 – Juneteenth

Commemorates the end of slavery on June 19, 1865. Major General Gordon Granger landed at Galveston, Texas with news that the war had ended and that the enslaved were free two and a half years after Lincoln signed the Emancipation Proclamation on January 1, 1863.
https://blogs.loc.gov/loc/2015/06/celebrating-juneteenth/

June 24 – Ramadan Ends

July

July 4 – Independence Day

July 14 – Bastile Day – France

July 18 – Nelson Mandela Day

August

August 12 – International Youth Day

September

Library Card Signup Month

http://www.ala.org/news/mediapresscenter/factsheets/librarycardsign

September 8 – International Literacy Day

September 10 – Grandparents Day

Host a grandparents day highlighting grandparents from various cultures and include song, music, and food of the cultures of the grandparents visiting.
https://grandparentsday.org/

September 15 – October 15 – Hispanic American History Month

http://hispanicheritagemonth.gov/

http://www.loc.gov/teachers/classroommaterials/primarysourcesets/hispanic-exploration/
Library of Congress Primary Source- Hispanic Exploration in America

http://www.nea.org/tools/lessons/hispanic-heritage-month.html

http://www.loc.gov/teachers/classroommaterials/primarysourcesets/mexican-americans/
Library of Congress Primary Source- Mexican Americans Migrations and Communities

September 20 -22 Rosh Hashana

September 21 – Islamic New Year

September 21 – International Day of Peace

September 24 – 30 – Banned Books Week

September 27 – Banned Websites Awareness

September 30 – Yom Kippur

October

Teen Read Week

http://teenreadweek.ning.com/

National Italian American heritage Month

October 1 – World Vegetarian Day

October 6 – German American Day

October 16 – World Food Day

October 24 – United Nations Day

October 31 – November 2 – Dia de Los Muertos (Day of the Dead)

November

Picture Book Month

National Native American Heritage Month

http://nativeamericanheritagemonth.gov/
https://www.whitehouse.gov/the-press-office/2016/10/31/
presidential-proclamation-national-native-american-heritage-month-2016

November 19 – International Games Day

November 11 – Veteran's Day

November 16 – International Day for Tolerance

November 23 – Thanksgiving

December

December 12 –20 Hanukkah

http://www.history.com/topics/holidays/hanukkah

December 25 – Christmas

http://www.history.com/topics/christmas

December 26 – Boxing Day

http://www.history.com/news/ask-history/why-is-the-day-after-christmas-called-boxing-day

December 26 -January 1 -Kwanzaa

http://www.officialkwanzaawebsite.org/index.shtml

> *"We need to help students and parents cherish and preserve the ethnic and cultural diversity that nourishes and strengthens this community – and this nation."*
>
> — *Cesar Chavez*

EBooks

Distributor	Overview	URL
Follett/Follett Shelf	Hosted virtual bookshelf that provides access to digital content	https://www.fes.follett.com/follettshelf/index.cfm
Mackin/ Mackinvia	Digital resource management system for eBooks, audio books, databases, and videos	https://www.mackin.com/corp/
Overdrive	Digital distributor of eBooks, audio books, videos, and music	https://www.overdrive.com/
Solution		
Epic	Free eBooks; creates individualized recommendations based on interest and reading level	https://www.getepic.com/
Scholastic Storia	Digital subscription; provides unlimited simultaneous access to eBooks for grades Pre-K – 6.Also provides customizable reports	http://www.scholastic.com/storia-school/
Bookflix	Interactive literacy resource that pairs fictional videos from Weston Woods with nonfiction eBooks from Scholastic	http://www.scholastic.com/digital/
Tumble Books	Animated, talking picture books that include sound, music, and narration	http://www.tumblebooklibrary.com/Default.aspx?ReturnUrl=%2f
Brain Hive	eBook collections for school and libraries; pay-per-use model	http://www.brainhive.com/Pages/Home.aspx
Open Ebooks	Free eBooks for Title I schools	http://openebooks.net/

Solution		
Bookshare	Bookshare® membership is for people with print disabilities and is provided FREE to U.S. students of any age and school;non-students and other organizations pay a low fee	https://www.bookshare.org
Gale Virtual Reference Library	EBooks on varied subjects, reference works, and nonfiction	http://www.cengage.com/search/showresults.do?N=197+4294904997
Project Gutenberg	Offers over 53,000 free eBooks	http://www.gutenberg.org/wiki/Main_Page
Story Line Online	The SAG-AFTRA Foundation records well-known actors reading children's books and makes graphically dynamic videos so that children around the world can be read to with just the click of a Storyline Online video book image	http://www.storylineonline.net/

Ebook Solutions

eBooks are a great way to offer diversity in your collection. eBooks can help struggling readers. Various features of eBooks offer an even more personalized reading experience for learners—for example, highlighting and note taking features, embedded multimedia with graphics, animation and video, and pronunciation and/or language translation. This ultimately supports learners as they build their vocabulary and reading comprehension skills. There are many options available. A chart appears at the end of this section to provide brief information about vendors. Many listed offer diverse titles and services to help you curate lists.

http://openebooks.net/getstarted.html
Open eBooks is a non-profit organization that provides new books and educational resources for free or at low cost to schools and programs serving children in need, from birth to age 18.Open eBooks is an app that contains thousands of popular and award-winning titles that are free for children from in-need households.

The app is available to low-income youth, special education classrooms, and children in military families. Any educator—teachers, program leaders, or librarians—may sign up and request access codes through First Book. Title I school wide programs whose districts utilize Clever can ask their district administrator to enable Open eBooks in their dashboard.

Free resources are great! With that said, if paying for a service is an option for you, this may allow you to build your collection more efficiently. Professional assistance may be just what you need to make the process less arduous. Consider working with vendors that support school libraries such as Follett School Solutions, Mackin, or Baker and Taylor to curate lists for purchase. You can provide these vendors with the topics you need and they will create custom lists for you.

eBook platforms that provide eBooks on a wide range of diverse topics for a fee may also give you the options you need. Fees are associated with some of the providers listed in the chart above.

Need Funds?

No money for these types of platforms? No problem. Consider the following options.

PTA Support/Donation

Approach your parent teacher organization and ask for a donation. Present what your collection's present stats are and then provide a clear picture of where you are trying to go. For example, share that only 5% of your total collection represents diverse titles. Your goal for the next 24 months is to build a collection that contains at least 15% diverse titles.

Individual Donation

Appeal to individuals within your school and community to donate funds to purchase eBooks.

Corporate Sponsors

Engage corporations in your city by inviting them into your school library to participate in a special program or to just observe for a day. Request that corporations make donations or purchase eBook platforms for the school. Be sure to express the benefits of maintaining a diverse eBook collection for your school. Offer to proudly display the corporation's logo on your webpage and in your media center. Publish the corporation's sponsorship in your school's newsletter and/or in the local newspaper.

Promote Your Diverse Library School Collection

Once you have created a diverse collection, promote it by creating catchy online newsletters and flyers for free with SMORE. Use SMORE to highlight different programs and features of your library's collection. SMORE's free plan offers 200 monthly emails and no custom background. The free version is a great way to learn the tool and determine if it's right for you. Additional options are available for a fee, and SMORE offers a special pricing plan for educators, $59 per year. You can link the SMORE to your library's webpage and/or the school's webpage. Send a SMORE directly to teachers and staff via email or to parents via mail. You can easily share SMORE on Facebook, Twitter, and other social media outlets.

What do you feature in your SMORE?

New additions to your collection

Highlight new books that you have recently acquired. Include a synopsis of the book and short biography of the author. This can be a recurring item that you include monthly.

Activities from your program

Highlight activities from the previous month and include photos. Be sure to follow your district's guidelines for using students' photos and always obtain written parental permission.

Calendar of upcoming events

Publish a calendar of upcoming events, such as an author visit, bake sale, or book fair. Include the particulars in the SMORE.

Solicit new volunteers

Use your SMORE as a vehicle to obtain new parent and community volunteers. Request help and be specific about your needs: whether this is monetary donations, hands to help reshelve books, or parents to speak about their culture and backgrounds.

Feature student work

Share poems, essays, or links to videos and podcasts for the community to see. This is an excellent way to share student work and give students an authentic audience that is wider than the teacher and their classmates. Remember to include all students from various backgrounds and ability levels.(Again follow your district's policy for posting students' work to the Internet.)

Create your free account and get started promoting your diverse school library program today.

SMORE

https://www.smore.com/educators

Publishers to Note

Lee and Low Books is the largest multicultural children's book publisher in the United States. This publisher warrants a closer look. Their website states they are an "independent children's book publisher specializing in diversity. It is the company's goal to meet the need for stories that children of color can identify with and that all children can enjoy. LEE & LOW makes a special effort to work with artists of color, and takes pride in nurturing many authors and illustrators who are new to the world of children's book publishing."[13]

Lee and Low publishes picture books as well as titles for middle grades and young adults. Lee and Low has the following imprints:

Bebop Books

Books for beginning readings in guided reading and intervention settings
https://www.leeandlow.com/imprints/2

Shen's Books

Concentrates on cultural diversity and tolerance; focuses on the different cultures of Asia
https://www.leeandlow.com/imprints/5

Dive Into Reading

Beginning chapter books
https://www.leeandlow.com/imprints/7

---

[13] Lee and Low. https://www.leeandlow.com (accessed November 1, 2016).

Tu Books

Middle grades and young adult novels that feature diverse characters and settings
https://www.leeandlow.com/imprints/3

Children's Book Press

By and about people of color; focuses on the Latino experience
https://www.leeandlow.com/imprints/4

Lee & Low Games

Games in literacy, math, and critical thinking
https://www.leeandlow.com/imprints/6
The Lee and Low website features an educator section that houses teacher guides and lesson plans. Additionally, it features extensive title lists for diverse readers, articles, activities, and much more.

Lee and Low Books logo reprinted with permission.

New Titles from Lee and Low Publisher

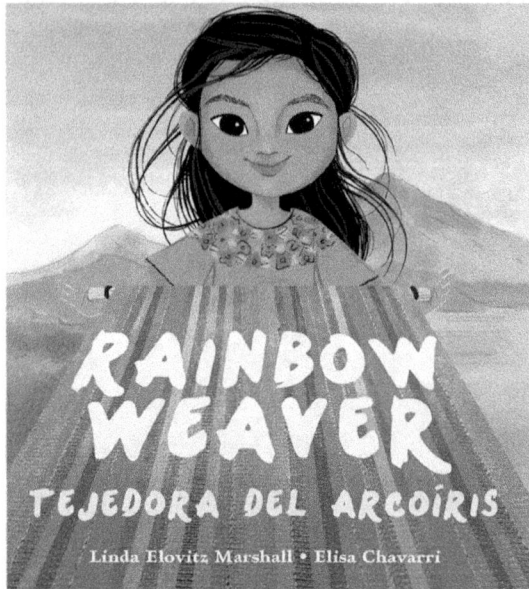

Rainbow Weaver/Tejedora del arcoíris

By Linda Elovitz Marshall
Illustrated by Elisa Chavarri

ISBN:

Hardcover: 9780892393749

Interest Level: Grades K – 4

Bilingual story that highlights the Mayan art of weaving.

https://www.leeandlow.com/books/2939

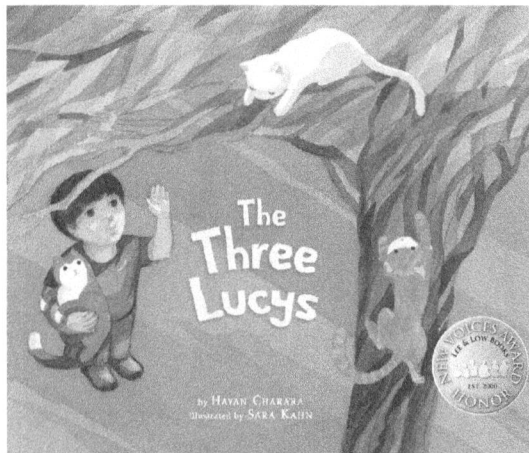

The Three Lucys

By HayanCharara
Illustrated by Sara Kahn

ISBN

Hardcover: 9781600609985

Interest Level: Grades 2 – 7

The Three Lucys is inspired by real events of the July War in Lebanon. This story of loss, rebuilding, and healing is a tribute to the sustaining love of family and to the power of the human spirit to hope for a peaceful future.

https://www.leeandlow.com/books/2935

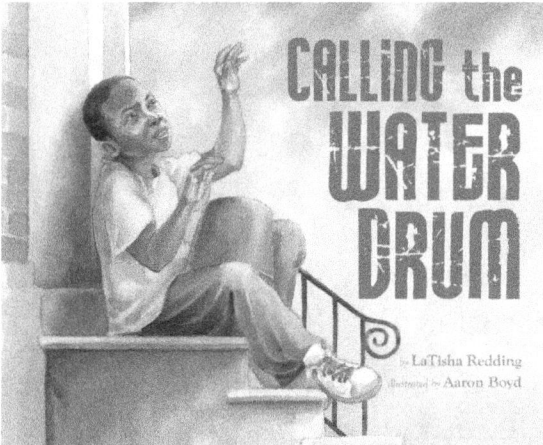

Calling the Water Drum

By LaTisha Redding
Illustrated by Aaron Boyd

ISBN

Hardcover: 9781620141946

Interest Level: Grades PreK – 5

Story of a Haitian boy's resilience and ability to start life anew in America.

https://www.leeandlow.com/books/2940

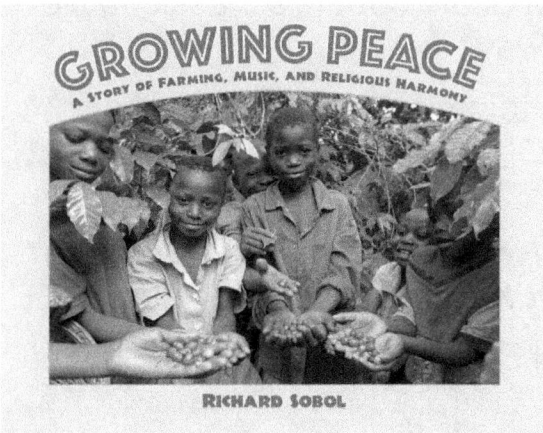

Growing Peace: A Story of Farming, Music, and Religious Harmony

Written and photographed by Richard Sobol

ISBN

Hardcover: 9781600604508

Interest Level: Grades 2 – 7

Photo-essay that is a timely story of hope, economic cooperation, and religious harmony from an often struggling part of the world. Story highlights people from different religions working together in Uganda.

https://www.leeandlow.com/books/2938/reviews/3007

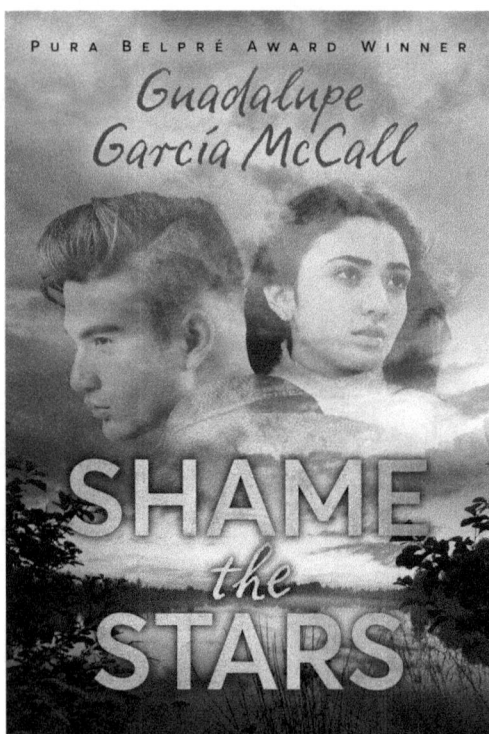

Shame the Stars

By Guadalupe Garcia McCall

ISBN

Hardcover: 9781620142783

E-Book: 9781620142790

Interest Level: Grades 7 – 12

Shame the Stars is a rich reimagining of Romeo and Juliet set in Texas during the explosive years of Mexico's revolution. Filled with period detail, captivating romance, and political intrigue, it brings Shakespeare's classic to life in an entirely new way.

Book synopsishttps://www.leeandlow.com/books/2934

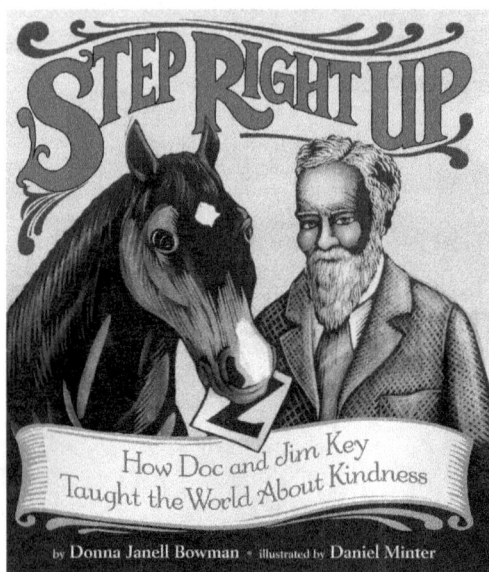

Step Right Up: How Doc and Jim Key Taught the World About Kindness

By Donna Janell Bowman

ISBN

Hardcover: 9781620141489

Interest Level: Grades 2 – 6

True story of an extraordinary horse and the remarkable man who nurtured the horse's natural abilities. Together they asked the world to step right up and embrace their message of kindness toward animals.

Book synopsis https://www.leeandlow.com/books/2937

Cover art reprinted with permission from Lee & Low Books.

Second Story Press

https://secondstorypress.ca/ is dedicated to publishing feminist-inspired books for adults
and young readers.Their titles accent strong female characters and delve into themes
of social justice, human rights, equality, and ability issues.

Second Story Press

New Releases – Children's Books

As A Boy by Plan International

ISBN: 9781772600162
Ages 5-9/Grades 1-3

This title features photographs paired with text to convey the message that boys matter.

The publisher's website features an ESL teaching guide to accompany the book.

Being Me by Rosemary McCarney

ISBN: 9781927583937
Ages 4-7/Grades 1-3

Rosie the Red learns that she doesn't have to wait until she's a grown up to be able to make a difference for others when she volunteers at a food bank (Synopsis from https://secondstorypress.ca/kids/being-me)

Second Story Press logo reprinted with permission.

I am Not A Number by Jenny Kay Dupuis and Kathy Kacer

ISBN: 9781927583944
Ages 7-11/Grades 3-6

Indigenous educator Dr. Jenny Kay Dupuis teams up with author Kathy Kacer to tell a true and personal story of Canada's residential school past. (Synopsis from https://secondstorypress.ca/kids/i-am-not-a-number)

The Mask That Sang by Susan Currie

ISBN: 9781772600131
Ages 9-13/Grades 5-7

A young girl discovers her Cayuga heritage when she finds a mask that sings to her. The publisher's website features an ESL teaching guide to accompany the book.

The Ship to Nowhere: On board the Exodus by Rona Arato

ISBN: 9781772600186

This book is a part of the A Holocaust Remembrance Book for Young Readers

It is the story of Rachel and her family, along with thousands of other Jewish refugees after the Holocaust, and their journey board the Exodus—a ship bound for Palestine. (Synopsis from https://secondstorypress.ca/kids/the-ship-to-nowhere)

New Releases – Teen Books

Don't Tell, Don't Tell, Don't Tell byLiane Shaw

ISBN: 9781927583951
Ages 12-16/Grades 8-12

A novel told from the perspectives of a teenage boy with Asperger's Syndrome and a teenage girl dealing with sexual assault.https://secondstorypress.ca/teen/dont-tell-dont-tell-dont-tell

Freedom's Just Another Word by Caroline Stellings

ISBN: 9781772600117
Ages 12-16/Grades 7-10

Tells the story of Easy, a gifted blues singer, and her journey as she meets Janis Joplin, a famous and addicted rock-blues singer.https://secondstorypress.ca/teen/freedoms-just-another-word

My Demon's Name is Ed by Danah Khalil

ISBN: 9781927583968
Ages 12-16/Grades 7-10

An eighteen year old author shares a teen's journal that reveals her struggle as her eating disorder becomes the overwhelming voice in her head. The book is based on the author own life's struggles. https://secondstorypress.ca/teen/my-demons-name-is-ed

The Pain Eater by Beth Goobie

ISBN: 9781772600209
Ages 13-17/Grades 8-12

This novel addresses the life of girls dealing with sexual abuse. It also deals with topics such as cyber bullying, gender stereotypes, and rape. This novel addresses timely gender issues of both males and females.

Susanna Moodie: Roughing It in the Bush by Carol Shields and Patrick Crowe

ISBN: 9781772600032
Ages 13-18/Grades 8-12

Graphic novel about a pioneer woman in 19th century Canada, Susanna Moodie, who was also a romantic writer. The publisher's website features an ESL teaching guide to accompany the book. https://secondstorypress.ca/teen/susanna-moodie

Stephanie Perry Moore

The Payton Skky Series was the first African American Christian teen series written by Stephanie Perry Moore. Her titles feature African American teens as main characters and offer inspiration. Stephanie Perry Moore is the author of several series and many titles.

Her series include:

Urban Flip Book Series
The Swoop List
Lockwood Lions
NEW Suburban Flip Book Series
Grovehill Giants
Payton Skky Series
Laurel Shadrach Series
Perry Skky Jr. Series
Yasmin Peace Series
Faith Thomas Novelzine Series
Carmen Browne Series
Morgan Love Series
Beta Gamma Pi Series

For more information visit http://www.stephanieperrymoore.com/

Plan International Canada Books

Because I am a Girl I Can Change the World

by Rosemary McCarney with Jen Albaugh and Plan International
ISBN: 9781927583449
Ages 8-14/Grades 4-7

Everyday is Malala Day

by Rosemary McCarney and Plan International
ISBN: 9781927583319
Ages 5-8/Grades 1-3

The Way to School

by Rosemary McCarney and Plan International
ISBN: 9781927583784
Ages 6-9/Grades 1-3

*Plan International is an international charity that works to end global poverty. It is a not-for-profit working to improve the lives of all children, independent and inclusive of all faiths and cultures.

The Kids Making A Difference Series

Our Heroes: How Kids Are Making A Difference

by Janet Wilson
ISBN: 9781927583418
Ages 7-12/Grades 3-6

Our Rights: How Kids Are Changing the World

by Janet Wilson
ISBN: 9781926920955
Ages 7-12/Grades 3-6

Our Earth: How Kids Are Saving the Planet

by Janet Wilson
ISBN: 9781897187845
Ages 7-12/Grades 3-6

The Gutsy Girls Series

Connecting Dots

by Sharon Jennings
ISBN: 9781927583623
Ages 8-12/Grades 5-7

The Contest

by Caroline Stellings
ISBN: 9781897187647
Ages 8-12/Grades 3-6

Finding Grace

by Becky Citra
ISBN: 9781927583258
Ages 9-12/Grades 4-6

Home Free

by Sharon Jennings
ISBN: 978897187555
Ages 8-12/Grades 3-6

Nikki Haydon Mysteries

The Scratch on the Ming Vase

by Caroline Stellings
ISBN: 9781926920917
Ages 12-16/Grades 7-11

The Secret of the Flower Garden

by Caroline Stellings
ISBN: 9781927583630
Ages 12-16/Grades 7-10

The Rachel Trilogy

Rachel's Secret

by Shelly Sanders
ISBN: 9781926920375
Ages 13-17/Grades 8-12

Rachel's Promise

by Shelly Sanders
ISBN: 9781927583142
Ages 13-18/Grades 8-12

Rachel's Hope

by Shelly Sanders
ISBN: 9781927583425
Ages 13-17/Grades 8-12

Additional information for series available at https://secondstorypress.ca/series/

Authors with DisAbilities

The following authors with disabilities appeared in a featured round table discussion on the *We Need Diverse Books* website.[14]

The featured authors were Corinne Duyvis, Sarah Jae-Jones, Tara Kelly, Kody Keplinger, Cindy L. Rodriguez, and Francisco X. Stork.

These authors offer a great starting place when discussing literature by authors with disabilities. One thing to keep in mind is that literature by authors with disabilities is not just for students with disabilities. These works can and should be read by a wide audience.

Corinne Duyvis:

Author http://www.corinneduyvis.net/

Titles

Guardians of the Galaxy: Collect Them All Release date April 2017 [Science Fiction]
On the Edge of Gone [Fantasy]
Otherbound [Science Fiction]

Sarah Jae-Jones:

Author https://sjaejones.com/

Title

Wintersong: A Novel [Fantasy]

Tara Kelly:

Author http://thetaratracks.com/

---

[14] We Need Diverse Books. 2016. "Perspectives of Authors with Disabilities – Part 1." <http://weneeddiversebooks.org/perspectives-of-authors-with-disabilities-part-1/>(accessed December 6, 2016).

Titles

Encore
Amplified
The Foxglove Killings
Harmonic Feedback

Kody Keplinger:

Author http://www.kodykeplinger.com/

Titles

Young Adult
Run
Lying Out Loud
Designated Ugly Fat Friend
Secret & Lies
A Midsummer Nightmare
Shut Out
Middle Grades
The Swift Boys and Me

Cindy L. Rodriguez:

Author https://cindylrodriguez.com/

Title

When Reason Breaks

Francisco X. Stork:

Author http://www.franciscostork.com/

Titles

The Way of the Jaguar [Fiction]
Behind the Eyes [Fiction]
Marcelo in the Real World [Fiction]
The Last Summer of the Death Warriors [Fiction]
Irises [Fiction]
The Memory of Light [Fiction]

Calendar of Diversity

Suggested Titles to Read Monthly

January

Martin Luther King Day

Martin Luther King Jr. in His Own Words

By Ryan Nagelhout
The book features Martin Luther King's own writings and speeches.
ISBN: 9781482401479
Interest Level: Grades 3 – 5
Publisher: Gareth Stevens Publishing

Martin Luther King and the March on Washington

By Stephanie Watson

Explores the events that led up to the March on Washington in 1963

ISBN: 9781624038815

Interest Level: Grades 3 – 4

Publisher: Core Library

It's Chinese New Year

By Richard Sebra

Book explains the holiday and traditions of the Chinese New Year.

ISBN: 9781512414257

Interest Level: Grades K – 2

Publisher: Lerner Publications

February

African American History Month

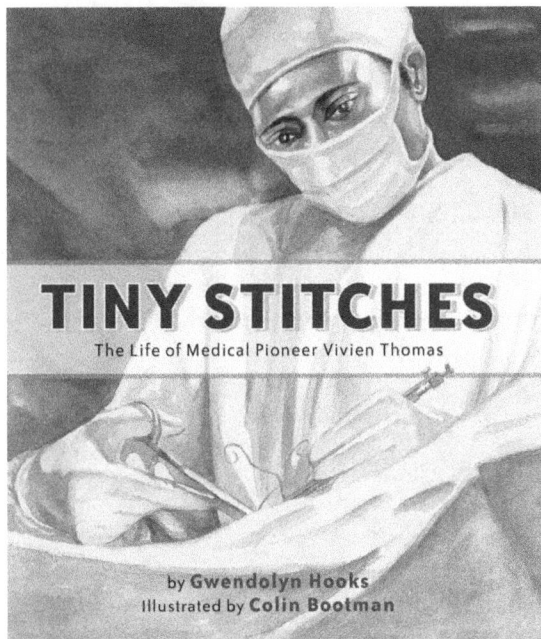

Tiny Stitches: The Life of Medical Pioneer Vivien Thomas

By Gwendolyn Hudson Hooks
Illustrated by Colin Bootman

Biography of Viven Thomas

ISBN

Hardcover: 9781620141564

Interest Level: Grades 2 – 8

Publisher: Lee and Low Books

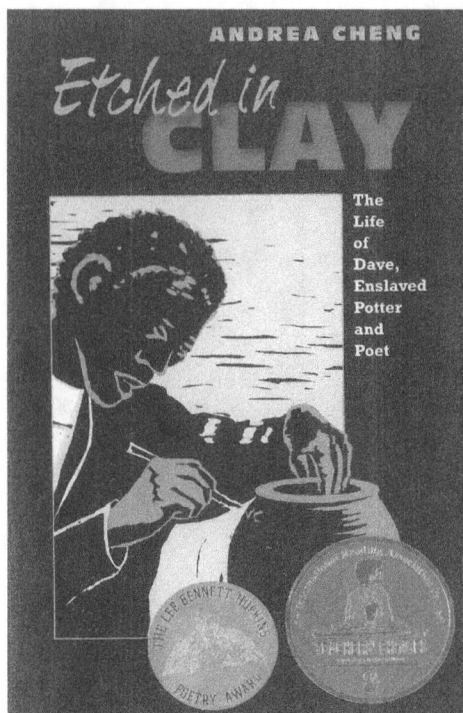

Etched in Clay: The Life of Dave, Enslaved Potter and Poet

Biography of an enslaved man

ISBN: 9781600604515

Interest Level: Grades 4 – 6

Publisher: Lee and Low Books

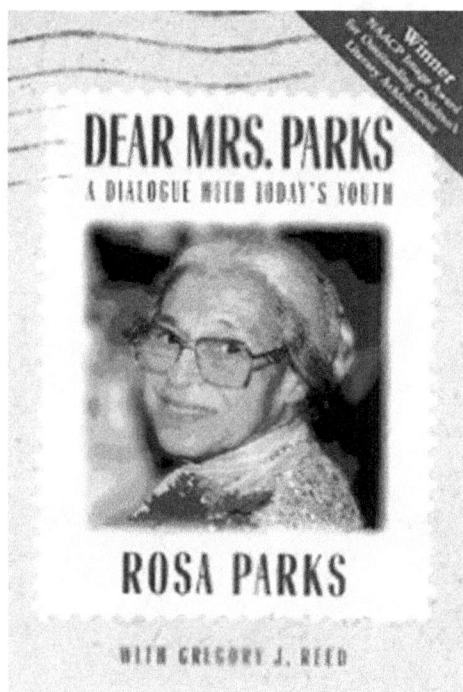

Dear Mrs. Parks: a

By Rosa Parks

Collection of letters from children and Mrs. Park's response to those letters.

ISBN

Paperback: 9781880000618

Hardcover: 9781880000458

Interest Level: Grades 1 – 5

Publisher: Lee and Low Books

In the Shadow of Liberty: the Hidden History of Slavery, Four Presidents, and Five Black Lives

By Kenneth Davis

The true story of five slaves and their presidential owners.

ISBN: 9781627793117

Interest Level: Grades 4 – 12

Publisher: Henry Holt and Company

28 Days: Moments in Black History that Changed the World

By Charles R. Smith

Collection of biographies on such African Americans as Harriet Tubman, Madame C. J. Walker and many more.

ISBN: 9781596438200

Interest Level: Grades 2 – 5

Publisher: Roaring Book Press

March: Book One
ISBN: 9781603093002

March: Book Two
ISBN: 9781603094009

March: Book Three

ISBN: 9781603094023

By John Lewis & Andrew Aydin
Illustrator Nate Powell

Graphic novel that presents John Lewis life and struggles in the Civil Rights Movement.

Interest Level: Grades 8 – 12

Publisher: Top Shelf Productions

March

Women's History Month

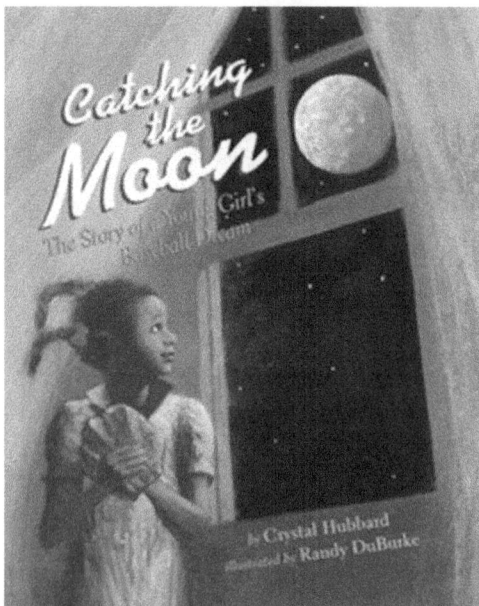

Catching the Moon: The Story of a Young Girl's Baseball Dream

By Crystal Hubbard
Illustrated by Randy DuBurke

The story of a young woman who grew up to become the first female to play for an all make baseball team.

ISBN

Paperback: 9781600605727

Hardcover: 9781584302438

Interest Level: Grades 1 – 5

Publisher: Lee and Low Books

https://www.leeandlow.com/books/catching-the-moon

Shining Star: The Anna May Wong Story

By Paula Yoo
Illustrated by Lin Wan

The story of Anna May Wong the first Chinese American movie star.

ISBN

Hardcover: 9781600602597

Paperback: 9781620142578

Interest Level: Grades 1 – 6

Publisher: Lee and Low Books

https://www.leeandlow.com/books/shining-star

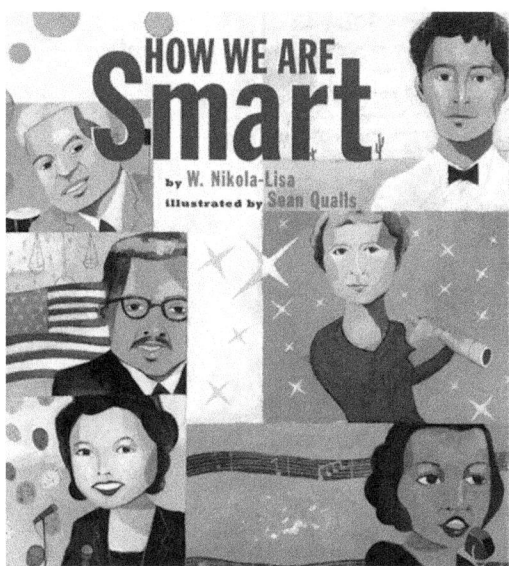

How We Are Smart

By W. Nikola-Lisa

Illustrated by Sean Qualls

Book features biographies of persons who have excelled in various intelligences.

ISBN

Paperback: 9781600604447

Hardcover: 9781584302544

Interest Level: Grades 1 – 8

Publisher: Lee and Low Books

https://www.leeandlow.com/books/64/pb/how_we_are_smart

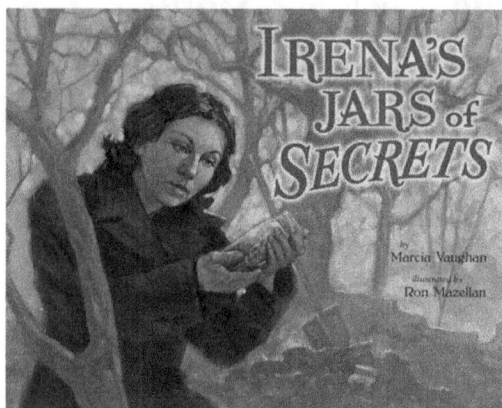

Irena's Jars of Secrets

By Marcia Vaughan
Illustrated by Ron Mazellan

Picture book biography of Irena Polish Catholic social worker credited with helping to save the lives of hundreds of children.

ISBN

Hardcover: 9781600604393

Paperback: 9781620142523

Interest Level: Grades 2 – 7

Publisher: Lee and Low Bookshttps://www.leeandlow.com/books/2759

Hidden Figures: The American Dream and The Untold Story of the Black Women Mathematicians Who Helped Win the Space Race

By Lee Shetterly, Margot

Story about the African American women mathematicians who were critical to the success of NASA's space program.

ISBN: 9780062363596

Interest Level: Grades 5 – 12

Publisher: Morrow

Life in Motion: An Unlikely Ballerina: Young Readers Edition

By Misty Copeland

Autobiography of Misty Copeland, the first African American Principal Ballerina in the American Ballet Theatre. She tells the story of her struggles and rise to fame.

ISBN: 9781481479790

Interest Level: Grades 4 – 7

Publisher: Aladdin

Trailblazers: 33 Women in Science Who Changed the World

By Rachel Swaby

The story of thirty women who made significant contributions in science. Women in astronomy, biology, medicine and technology are featured.

ISBN: 9780399553967

Interest Level: Grades 4 – 8

Publisher: Delacorte Press

Zero Discrimination Day

HIV/AIDS

By Kathy Furgang

Discusses HIV infections and AIDS

ISBN: 9781499460667

Interest Levels: Grades 10 – 12

Publisher: Rosen Publishing

Positive: Surviving My Bullies, Finding Hope, and Living to Change the World: A Memoir

By Paige Rawl

Autobiography of a teen living HIV positive

ISBN: 9780062342515

Interest Levels: Grades 6 – 12

Publisher: Harper Collins

Cesar Chavez Day

Cesar Chavez

By Christine Juarez

Biography written for young readers about the life of Cesar Chavez

ISBN: 9781515718925

Interest Levels: Grades PreK – 2

Publisher: Capstone Press

Cesar Chavez

By Josh Gregory

ISBN: 9780531211724

Biography highlighting the life of Cesar Chavez, Mexican American Labor Leader

Interest Level: Grades 2 – 4

Publisher: Children's Press

April

Poetry Month

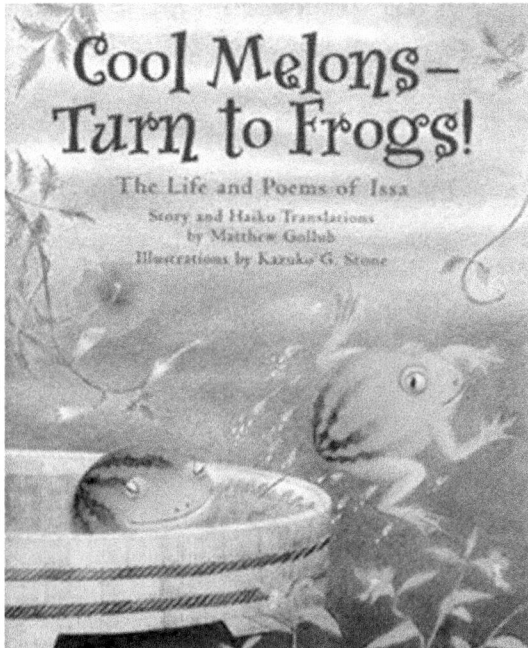

Cool Melons— Turn to Frogs! The Life and Poems of Issa

By Matthew Gollub
Illustrated by Kazuko G. Stone

Book about the life and poems of Issa, Japanese Haiku poet

ISBN

Paperback: 9781584302414

Hardcover: 9781880000717

Interest Level: Grades 1 – 6

Publisher: Lee and Low Books

https://www.leeandlow.com/books/2379

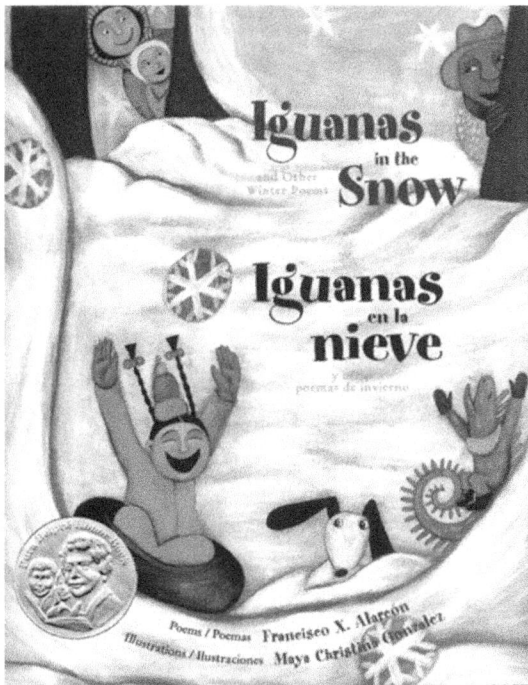

Iguanas in the Snow and Other Winter Poems/Iguanas en la nieve y otrospoemas de invierno

By Francisco Alarcón
Illustrated by Maya Christina Gonzalez

Book of poetry

ISBN

Paperback: 9780892392025

Interest Level: Grades 2 – 6

Publisher: Lee and Low Books
https://www.leeandlow.com/books/2793

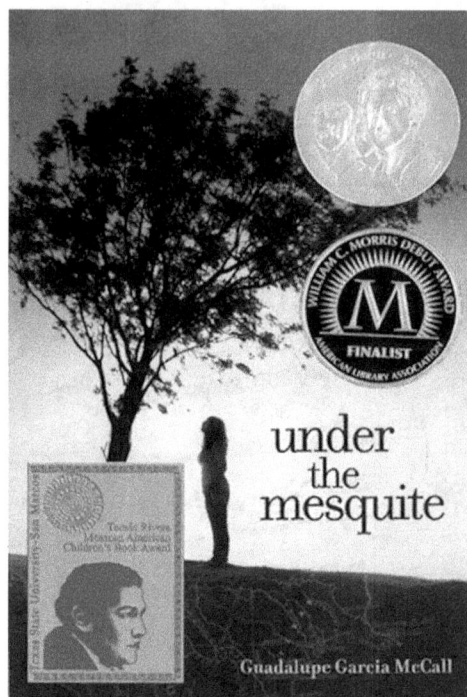

Under the Mesquite

By Guadalupe Garcia McCall

Novel written by Mexican American author about 14 year old's loss, family and courage.

ISBN

Hardcover: 9781600604294

Interest Level: Grades 6 – 12

Publisher: Lee and Low Books

https://www.leeandlow.com/books/under-the-mesquite

Strange Fruit: Billie Holiday and the Power of a Protest Song

By Gary Golio

This book chronicles the jazz song "Strange Fruit" and how the song focuses on lynching and racism in America.

ISBN: 9781467751230

Interest Level: Grades 2 – 6

Publisher: Millbrook Press

May

Rashad's Ramadan *and Eid al-Fitr*

By Lisa Bullard

Explains Ramadan and Eid al-Fitr, the history and customs.

ISBN: 9780761350798

Interest Level: Grades 1 -2

Publisher: Millbrook Press

Cinco de Mayo: Celebrating Mexican History and Culture

By Leia Tait

Explores the Cinco de Mayo holiday and presents Mexican history.

ISBN: 9781605967769

Interest Levels: Grades 4 – 6

Publisher: AV2 by Weigl

Asian Pacific American History Month

The Asian Pacific American Experience

By Karen Sirvaitis

Showcases the accomplishments of Asian Pacific Americans and presents their struggles.

ISBN: 9780761340898

Interest Levels: Grades 6 – 8

Publisher: Twenty First Century Books

June

Juneteenth

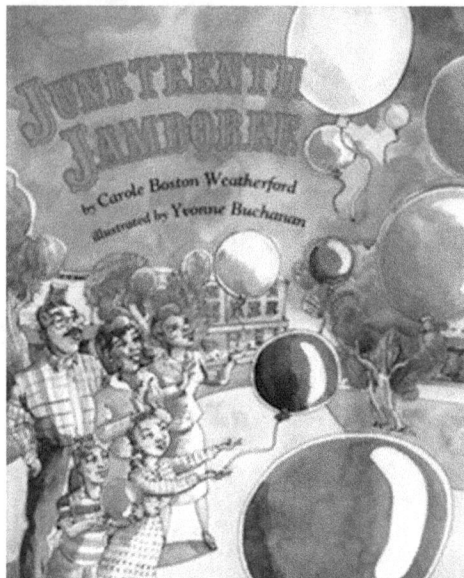

Juneteenth Jamboree

By Carole Boston Weatherford
Illustrated by Yvonne Buchanan

Story that informs the reader about Juneteenth

ISBN

Paperback: 9781600602481

Interest Level: Grades 1 – 5

Publisher: Lee and Low Books

https://www.leeandlow.com/books/juneteenth-jamboree

*Title also available in Spanish

¡Celebremos Juneteenth!

Glbt Book Month

Stonewall: Breaking Out in the Fight for Gay Rights

By Ann Bausum

The book explores the Stonewall raids and the struggle for gay rights in the United States

ISBN: 9780670016792

Interest Level: Grades 6 – 12

Publisher: Penguin Group USA

Jazz Jennings: Voice for LGBTQ Youth

By Ellen Rodger

ISBN: 9780778734192

Interest Level: Grades 6 – 12

Publisher: Crabtree Publishing

LGBTQ+ Athletes Claim the Field: Striving for Equality

By Kirstin Cronn-Mills

Presents the struggles LBGT athletes endure to gain acceptance and honor, collection of biographies.

ISBN: 9781467780124

Interest Levels: Grades 6 – 12

Publisher: Twenty First Century Books

Being Jazz: My Life As A (Transgender) Teen

By Jazz Jennings

Autobiography of Jazz Jennings

ISBN: 9780399554643

Interest Levels: Grades 6 – 12

Publisher: Crown

Transgender Role Models and Pioneers

By Barbara Penne

Presents persons who have made significant accomplishments in the arts, politics, entertainment and sports

ISBN: 9781508171850

Interest Level: 6 – 12

Publisher: Rosen

Transgender Rights and Protections

By Rebecca Klein

Examines the rights of the transgender community

Interest Level: 6 – 12

ISBN: 9781499464603

Publisher: Rosen

JULY

Nelson Mandela Day

Nelson Mandela and the End of Apartheid

By Gaines Rodriguez, Ann Graham

ISBN: 9780766073005

Interest Level: Grades 7 -9

Publisher: Enslow Publishing

Nelson Mandela From Prisoner to President

By Suzy Capozzi

ISBN: 9780375974670

Interest Level: Grades 3 – 4

Publisher: Random House

August

International Youth Day

I am Malala: How One Girl Stood Up for Education and Changed the World

By Malala Yousafzai

Malala tells her story of courage and how her efforts changed the world.

ISBN: 9780316327930

Interest Level: Grades 4 – 12

Publisher: Little Brown and Company

September

Library Card Sign Up Month

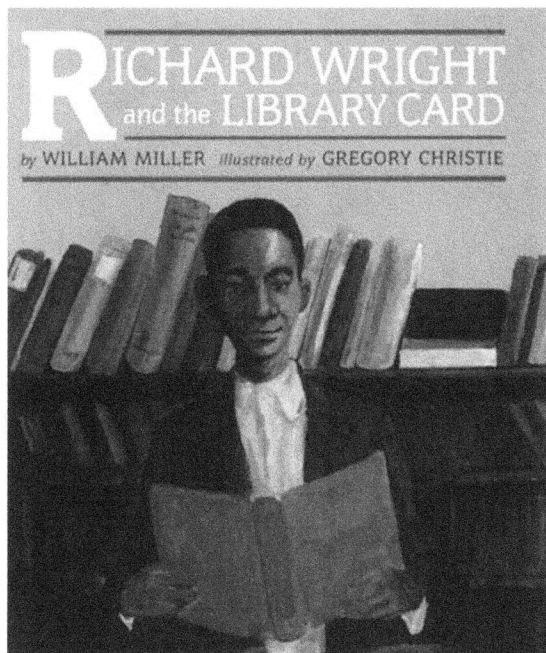

Richard Wright and the Library Card

By William Miller

ISBN

Paperback: 9781880000885

Hardcover: 9781880000571

Interest Level: Grades 2 – 6

Biography of Richard Wright

Publisher: Lee and Low Books
https://www.leeandlow.com/books/2441

International Literacy Day

Armando and the Blue Tarp School

By Edith Hope Fine and Judith Pinkerton Josephson

ISBN

Hardcover: 9781584302780

Paperback: 9781620141656

Interest Level: Grades K – 3

A story about chasing dreams and the power of one person to make a difference in the lives of others. Señor David sets up a blue tarp school on the playground and changes the lives of many.

Publisher: Lee and Low Books
https://www.leeandlow.com/books/2354

The Storyteller's Candle/La velita de loscuentos

By Lucía González

This work pays tribute to Pura Belpré, New York City's first Latina librarian.

ISBN

Paperback: 9780892392377

Hardcover: 9780892392223

Interest Level: Grades 1 – 6

Reading Level: Grades 3 – 4

Publisher: Lee and Low Books
https://www.leeandlow.com/books/2804

Hispanic Heritage Month

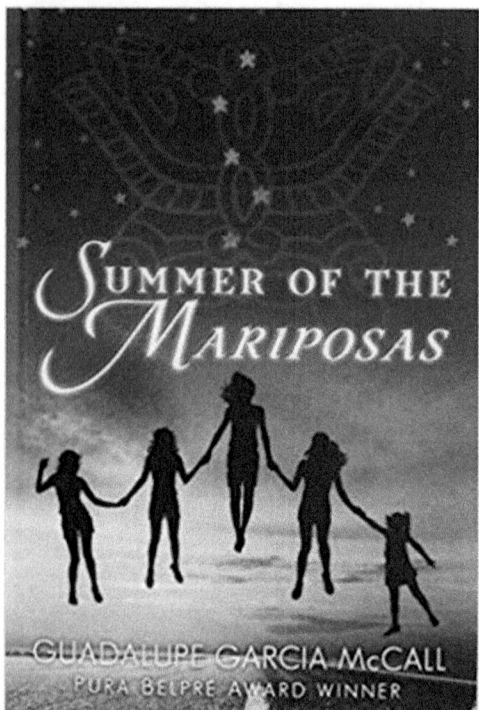

Summer of the Mariposas

By Guadalupe Garcia McCall

ISBN

Paperback: 9781620140109

Hardcover: 9781600609008

E-Book: 9781600609015

Interest Level: Grades 6 – College

Reading Level: Grades 5 – 6

Summer of the Mariposas is a Mexican American retelling of The Odyssey and a celebration of sisterhood and maternal love.

Publisher: Lee and Low Books
https://www.leeandlow.com/books/2811

Parrots Over Puerto Rico

By Susan L. Roth and Cindy Trumbore

ISBN

Hardcover: 9781620140048

Interest Level: Grades 1 – 6

Reading Level: Grades 4 – 5

This story details the work of the scientists of the Puerto Rican Parrot Recovery Program to save the parrots and ensure their future. It also included information about the history of Puerto Rico.

Publisher: Lee and Low Books
https://www.leeandlow.com/books/283

The Pot That Juan Built

By Nancy Andrews-Goebel

Juan Quezada is the premier potter in Mexico.

ISBN

Paperback: 9781600608483

Hardcover: 9781584300380

Interest Level: Grades 1 – 6

Publisher: Lee and Low Books
https://www.leeandlow.com/books/2434

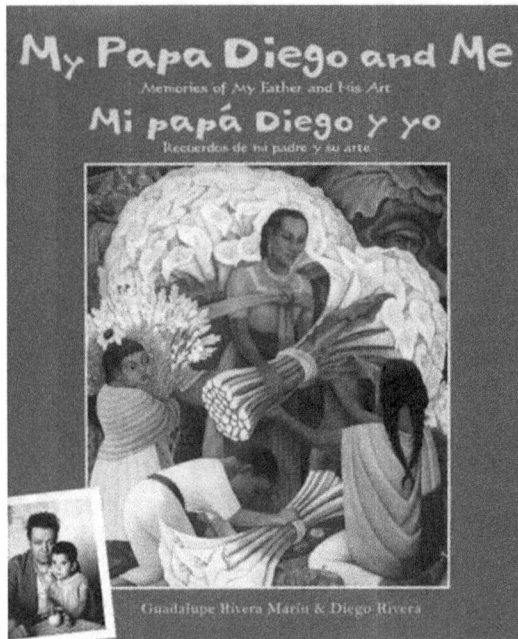

My Papa Diego and Me/Mipapá Diego y yo

By Guadalupe Marín

ISBN

Hardcover: 9780892392285

Paperback: 9780892393640

Interest Level: Grades 1 – 5

Reading Level: Grades 4 – 4

Guadalupe Rivera Marín shares some of her childhood memories of her world-renowned artist father, Diego Rivera.

Publisher: Lee and Low Books

Growing up Muslim: Understanding Islamic Beliefs and Practices

By Sumbul Ali-Karamali

Title presents Muslim beliefs and practices, offers information on beliefs and practices.

ISBN: 9780375989773

Interest Level: Grades 7 – 9

Publisher: Delacorte Press

Portraits of Hispanic American Heroes

By Juan Felipe Herrera

Collection of biographies of famous Hispanic Americans including artists, scientists, athletes and political leaders.

ISBN: 9780803738096

Interest Level: Grades 4 – 8

Publisher: Dial Books for Young Readers

OCTOBER

World Food Day

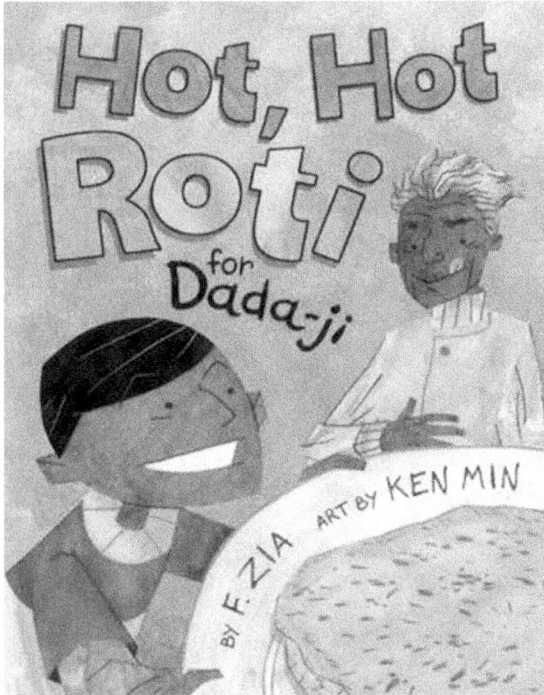

Hot, Hot Roti for Dada-ji

By F. Zia
Illustrated by Ken Min

ISBN

Hardcover: 9781600604430

Paperback: 9781620143520

Interest Level: Grades K – 5

Publisher: Lee and Low Books
https://www.leeandlow.com/books/
hot-hot-roti-for-dada-ji

Sweet Potato Pie

By Kathleen D. Lindsey
Illustrated by Charlotte Riley-Webb

ISBN

Paperback: 9781600602771

Hardcover: 9781584300618

Interest Level: Grades K – 3

Publisher: Lee and Low Books
https://www.leeandlow.com/books/
sweet-potato-pie

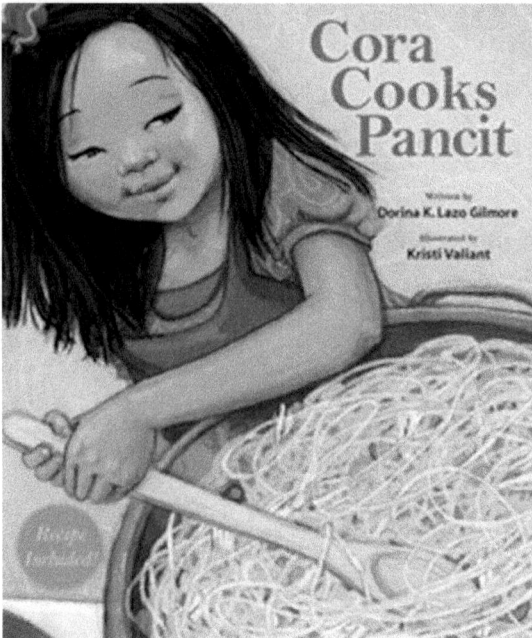

Cora Cooks Pancit

By DorinaLazo Gilmore
Illustrated by Kristi Valiant

ISBN

Paperback: 9781885008480

Interest Level: Grades K – 4

Publisher: Lee and Low Books
https://www.leeandlow.com/books/
cora-cooks-pancit

Day of the Dead

Day of the Dead

Julie Murray

ISBN: 9781624031823

Interest Level: Grades 2 – 3

Publisher: ADBO Publishing Company

November

Native American Heritage Month

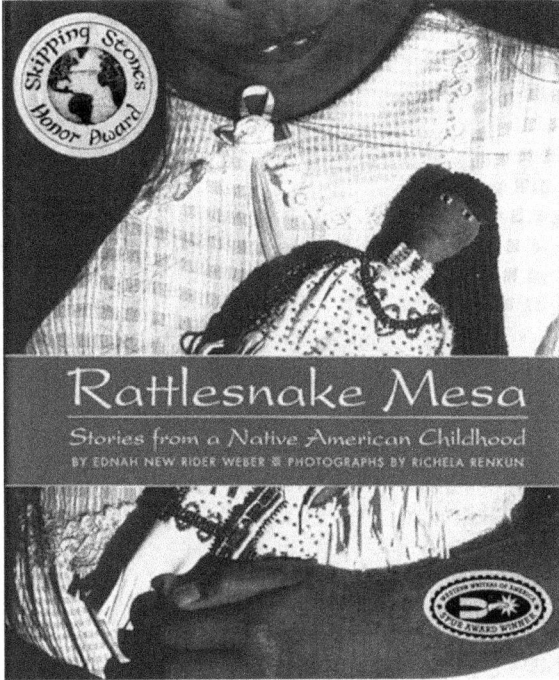

Rattlesnake Mesa: Stories from a Native American Childhood

By EdNah New Rider Weber

ISBN

Paperback: 9781600608742

Hardcover: 9781584302315

Interest Level: Grades 4 – 12

Reading Level: Grades 4 – 5

True accounts of a coming of age Pawnee girl.

Publisher: Lee and Low Books
https://www.leeandlow.com/books/2437

Wolf Mark

By Joseph Bruchac

ISBN

Hardcover: 9781600606618

E-Book: 978160060878

Interest Level: Grades 7 – 12

Joseph Bruchac is an Abenaki children's book author.

Publisher: Lee and Low Books
https://www.leeandlow.com/books/2755

Killer of Enemies

By Joseph Bruchac

ISBN

Hardcover: 9781620141434

E-Book: 9781620141441

Paperback: 9781620142769

Tale of seventeen-year-old Apache hunter, Lozen, of Abenaki and Apache ancestry. Lozen has powers and abilities and is forced to fight genetically altered monsters. This book is in the dystopian genre. Joseph Bruchac is an Abenaki children's book author.

Publisher: Lee and Low Books
https://www.leeandlow.com/books/2832

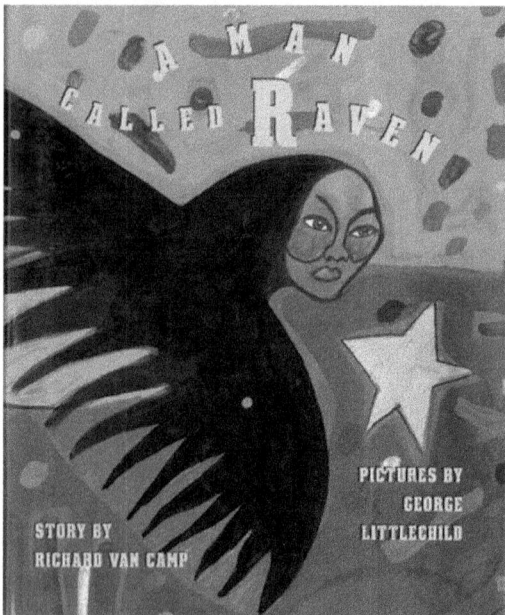

A Man Called Raven

By Richard Van Camp

ISBN

Hardcover: 9780892391448

Paperback: 9780892393053

Interest Level: Grades 2 – 5

Reading Level: Grades 3 – 3

A tribute to the wisdom of the raven and a positive reminder that we can all learn from nature.

Publisher: Lee and Low Books
https://www.leeandlow.com/books/2810

Bears Make Rock Soup

By Lise Erdrich

ISBN

Paperback: 9780892393008

Interest Level: Grades 3 – 5

Reading Level: Grades 3 – 4

A collection of paintings and stories that honor Native American tradition. The work pays tribute to the people, animals, forests, and river of the Plains.

Publisher: Lee and Low Books
https://www.leeandlow.com/books/2845

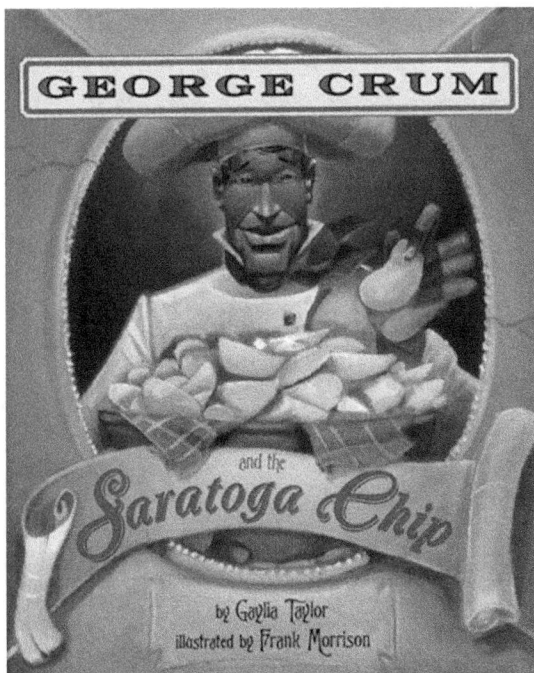

George Crum and the Saratoga Chip

By Gaylia Taylor

Story about the inventor of the potato chip.

ISBN

Paperback: 9781600606564

Hardcover: 9781584302551

Interest Level: Grades 1 – 5

Publisher: Lee and Low Books
https://www.leeandlow.com/books/2394

December

Kwanzaa

A Year Full of Stories

By Angela McAllister

Myths, fairy tales and legends from around the world. Stories are presented for all twelve months from around the world.

ISBN: 9781847808684

Interest Level: Grades K – 5

Publisher: Frances Lincoln Children's Books

Kwanzaa

By Lisa Herrington

Book about Kwanzaa

ISBN

Hardcover: 9780531272046

Paperback: 9780531273548

Interest Level: Pre K – 2

Publisher: Scholastic

Hanukkah

Hanukkah
By Lisa Herrington

Book about Hanukkah

ISBN

Hardback: 9780531272015

Paperback: 9780531273517

Interest Level: Pre K – 2

Publisher: Scholastic

All cover art reprinted with permission from Lee & Low Books. www.leeandlow.com

Additional Book Lists

Young Adult			
Homelessness			
Title	**Author**	**Publisher**	**Genre**
Breakfast at Sally's	Richard LeMieux, Michael Gordon	Skyhorse Publishing	Non fiction/ Autobiography
Beyond the Station Lises the Sea	Jutta Richter, Anna Brailovsky	Milkweed	Fiction
Everybody Can Help Somebody	Ron Hall, Denver Moore	Thomas nelson	Nonfiction/ Religious
	Katherin Applegate, Kirby Heybourne	Penguin	Fiction
On the Other Side of the Bridge	Ray Villareal	Arte Publico Press	Fiction/Latino
Trippin'	P J Gray	Saddleback Educational Publishers	Fiction/Urban
The Lab	P J Gray	Saddleback Educational Publishers	Fiction/Urban
Homelessness Comes to School	Joseph Murphy, Keei Tobin	Sage Publications	Nonfiction – Adult
Where Do You Stay	Andrea Cheng	Boyds Mill Press	Fiction
The Prince of Venice Beach	Blake Nelson	Little Brown Books for Young Readers	Fiction/Foster Homes
To Die For	Anne Schraff	Saddleback Educational Publishing	Fiction/Urban
Crash	Lesley Choyce	Orca Book Publishers	Fiction

Young Adult

Title	Author	Publisher	Genre
Homeless at Harvard: Fining Faith and Friendship on the Street of Harvard Square	John Frame	Zondervan	Autobiography/ Adult
Pieces of Me	Darlene Ryan	Orca Book Publishers	Fiction
Almost Home	Joan Bauer	Penguin Young Readers	Fiction

Differently-abled Characters and Authors

Title	Author	Publisher	Genre
Dead Girls Society	Michelle Krys	Random House	Fiction/Mystery
Our Chemical Hearts	Krystal Sutherland, Robbie Daymond	Penguin House Audio	Fiction/Romance
Shiny Broken Pieces	SonaCharaipotra, Dhonielle Clayton, Laura Delano, et. Al.	Harper Collins	Fiction
Love Blind	C. Desir, Jolene Perry	Simon & Schuster	Fiction/Romance
Not if I See You First	Eric Lindtrom	Little Brown Books for Young Readers	Fiction
Symptoms of Being Human	Jeff Garvin, Tom Phelan	Harper Collins	Fiction/LGBT
Other Broken Things	C. Desir	Simon & Schuster	Fiction
The Rest of Us Just Live Here	Patrick Ness, James Fouhey	Harper Collins	Fiction
Rules	Cynthia Lord, Jessica Almasy	Recorded Books	Fiction/Special Needs
The Sacred Lies of Minnow Bly	Stephanie Oakes	Penguin Group	Fiction
The Last Leaves Falling	Sarah Benwell	Simon & Schuster	Fiction/Suicide
Challenger Deep	Neal Shusterman, Michael Curran - Dorsano	Harper Collins	Fiction

Asian Teens

Title	Author	Publisher	Genre
Under the Lights	Dahlia Adler	Spencer Hill Contemporary	Fiction/LGBT
There Will Come A Time	Carrie Arcos	Simon Pulse	Fiction/Death & Dying
Something In Between	Melissa de la Cruz	Harlequin	Fiction
Eleanor & Park	Rainbow Rowell	St. Martin's Griffin	Fiction
Outrun the Moon	Stacey Lee	G.P. Putnam's Sons Books for Young Readers	Fiction/Historical
The Sun is Also A Star	Nicola Yoon	Delacorte Press	Fiction/Family Issues

African American

Author	Title	Publisher	Genre	Grades
Alexander, Kwame	The Crossover	HMH Books for Young Readers	Fiction	6 - 10
Asim, Jabari	Preaching to the Chickens: The Story of Young John Lewis	Nancy Paulsen Books	Nonfiction/ Picture Book	K - 5
Bolden, Tonya	Pathfinders: The Journeys of 16 Extraordinary Black Souls	Abrams Books for Young Readers	Collective Biogrpahy	5 - 8
Butler, Octavia Duffy, Damian & Jennings, John	Kindred: A Graphic Novel Adaptation	Harry N. Abrams	Historical Fiction - Graphic Novel	4 - 8
Giles, Lamar	Endangered	Harper Teen	Fiction - Suspense	9 - 12
Giles, Lamar	Fake ID	Harper	Fiction - Mystery	9 - 12
Giles, Lamar	Overturned	Scholastic Press	Fiction – Mystery	9-12
Grimes, Nikki	One Last Word: Wisdom from the Harlem Renaissance	Bloomsbury	Poetry	6 - 12
Hopkins, Deborah	Steamboat School	Disney Hyperion	Fiction - Historical	K - 3

Author	Title	Publisher	Genre	Grades
Jabbar, Kareem Abdul	Streetball Crew Series: Sasquatch in the Paint Stealing the Game	Disney Hyperion	Fiction	5 - 8
Jabbar, Kareem Abdul	What Color is My World? The Lost History of African American Inventors	Candlewick	Nonfiction/ Biogrpahical Fiction	3 - 6
Kaiser, Lisbeth	Maya Angelou (Little People, Big Dreams Series)	Frances Lincoln Children's Books	Biography	1 - 3
Lewis, John & Aydin, Andrew	March (Series)	Top Shelf Productions	Nonfiction – Graphic Novel / Autobiography	8 - 12
Magoon, Kekla	How It Went Down	Square Fish	Fiction	9 - 12
McKissack, Patricia	Let's Clap, Jump, Sing & Shout Dance, Spin& Turn It Out!	Penguin Random House	Nonfiction / Songs	2 - 6
Miles, Shanna	Willow Born	Rochelle Reed Publishing	Fiction	7 - 12
Reynolds, Jason	Ghost	Atheneum	Fiction	5 - 8
Reynolds, Jason & Kiely, Brendan	All American Boys	Atheneum	Fiction	9 - 12
Reynolds, Jason	Long Way Down	Atheneum	Fiction – to be released October 2017	8 - 12
Reynolds, Jason	The Boy in the Black Suit	Atheneum	Fiction	8 - 12
Steptoe, Javaka	Radiant Child – The Story of Young Artist Jean-Michael Basquiat	Little Brown & Company Books for Young Readers	Nonfiction – Biography/ Picture Book	1 - 5
Thomas, Angie	The Hate U Give	Balzer& Bray	Fiction	9 - 12
Young, Morgan	Lana and the Water Carrier	Fangirl Digital	Fiction	3 - 8

For The Little Ones

Author	Title	Grades	Subject	Publisher
Averbeck, Jim	One Word From Sophia	Pre K - 3	Shows diverse families in positive roles.	Atheneum
Bahk, Jane	Juna's Jar	Pre K – 2	Story of friendship and family interwoven with elements of Korean culture.	Lee & Low Books
Manushkin, Fran	Happy in Our Skin	Pre K– K	Straight forward representation of diversity in a picture book.	Candlewick Press
Peña, Matt de la	Last Stop on Market Street	K-2	Highlights diversity and an appreciation for difference.	Putnam's Sons
Medina, Meg	Mango, Abuela, and Me	K-3	The story of a Latina girl 's grandmother coming to live with the family in the United States.	Candlewick Press
O'Brien, Anne Sibley	I'm New Here	K-3	The story of new students from Guatemala, Somalia and Korea and their interactions at school.	Charlesbridge
Shannon, George	One Family	Pre K – 2	Represents diversity of family structures while integrating counting. (LGBTQ)	Farrar Straus Giroux
Thompson, Laurie Ann	Emmanuel's Dream: the True Story of Emmanuel OfosuYeboah	K-2	Biography about a Ghanaian boy born with physical challenges in one leg.	Schwartx& Wade Books

Hispanic

Author	Title	Publisher	Subject	Grades
Behar, Ruth	Lucky Broken Girl	Nancy Paulsen Books	Autobiographical Fiction	5 - 8
Cervantes, Angela	Allie, First at Last	Scholastic	Fiction	3 - 5
Cisneros, Sandra	House on Mango Street	Vintage	Fiction	6 - 12
Connolly, Daniel	The Book of Isaias: A Child of Hispanic Immigrnats Seeks His Own America	St. Martin	Fiction	9 - 12
Diamond, Jill	Lou Lou and Pea and the Mural Mystery	Farrar, Straus, Giroux	Fiction /Mystery	4 - 6
Engel, Margarita	Bravo: Poems about Amazing Hispanics	Henry Holt and Company	Collective Biographies / Poetry	4 - 7
Jules, Jacqueline	My Family Adventure (Series: Sofia Martinez)	Picture Window Books	Fiction	K - 2
Medina, Meg	Yaqui Delgado Wants to Kick Your Ass	Candlewick	Fiction	8 - 12
Ryan, Pam	Esperanza Rising	Scholastic	Fiction	6 - 9

Diverse Book Fairs

- Set a goal for your book fair: decide to provide access to as many diverse titles as possible. Make sure you have an adequate representation in terms of socio-economics, race, religion, geography, history, age, lifestyle, genres, gender, reading levels, ability, etc. reflected in the titles you have for sale.
- Ensure that titles by authors of color are available.
- If you are using a large, national book fair distributor, request that titles and authors reflect a broad spectrum of diversity.
- Work with local, independent bookstores in your area, if possible. Local stores may be more willing to personalize titles for your fair or work with you to make sure the titles reflect the diversity found in the world.
- Consider having a book fair in an actual bookstore, whether it is an independent store or a major retail outlet like Barnes and Noble. Make your fair more of a celebration and engage parents and the local community.
- Consider having an online book fair. As an example, Scholastic Book Fairs offer on online book fair. Send parents to the online book fair with customized lists that feature diverse titles.

http://www.scholastic.com/bookfairs/onlinefair

- When having an in-person book fair in your school library, highlight artifacts from various cultures by incorporating them as table displays.
- Serve food from various cultures to kick off the book fair or as part of a special shopping day or hour.
- Invite authors of diverse backgrounds to speak and offer their books for sale at your book fair. Get the authors to autograph copies and sell these copies along with a photo with the author for a slightly higher price. All proceeds benefit the library, of course.

Book fairs are a great way to generate excitement about the library and get parents in the door while generating funds for your program. With a little planning you can host a diverse book fair for your school!

Biblionasium

https://www.biblionasium.com

Social networking platform for students. Students can create reading logs, enter reading challenges, and share and discuss books. These can be shared with teachers, parents, and other students.

- Parents, teacher, and librarians can register students.
- Librarians can use this to build lists of diverse books and authors. This is a great way to guide students to more diverse titles.
- Reporting is available that details what students are reading.
- Destiny now offers integration with Biblionasium, offering a single sign on solution.

Age: 7 – 12
Cost: Free
COPPA (Child Online Privacy Protection Act) Compliant

Bookopolis

https://www.bookopolis.com/#/

Students can explore new books, create a bookshelf, and communicate with friends. Bookopolis tracks and promotes reading and writing through the use of badges and points. Books are rated and reviewed by others.

- Bookopolis does provide personalized reading recommendation based on what students have read.
- Students also practice persuasive writing, comprehension, and typing skills by completing reviews, reports, and reading logs online.

Age: 7 – 12
Cost: Free
COPPA (Child Online Privacy Protection Act) Compliant

DOGObooks

https://www.dogobooks.com

Books reviewed by and for children. This site hosted the YALSA 2016 Teens Top Ten. The site encourages teens to rate, review, and share books.

- This site hosted an online summer reading program in 2016.
- Integrates with Google and Clever.
- Requires students under the age of 13 to provide a parent or guardian's email address. All posts are reviewed before they are published.

Age: 7 – 17
Cost: Free
COPPA (Child Online Privacy Protection Act) Compliant

Goodreads

https://www.goodreads.com/

Excellent site to share information, make recommendations, review books, and track reading goals. Students can network socially with peers about what they are reading. While teachers can set up classroom groups, there is no method to create a "walled garden."The site does contain reviews, quizzes, and biographical information about authors. Students may be able to interact with adults. Adult content may be visible to students.

Age: Adult – Use with CAUTION with high school students
Cost: Free
Not COPPA Compliant

Maximum Reader Engagement with Instructional Technology Tools

Discovery Education

www.discoveryeducation.com

Discovery Education offers digital content, interactive lessons, virtual field trips, techbooks (digital text books), streaming content aligned to standards. Discovery also offers content collections which include content targeted around specific topics. For example, they feature a content collection on Black History Month for elementary, middle and high school which includes lesson starters, songs, audio, instructional strategies, video segments, images, lesson materials including quizzes, assignments, writing prompts, graphic organizers and links to encyclopedia articles.

- Discovery also provides a Board Builder which students can use to create online, multimedia projects.

Cost: Free and Paid premium content
Must have written parental permission for students under the age of 13.

Easel.ly

https://www.easel.ly/

Free online tool to create and share visual representations of ideas such as infographics and posters.

- Students can use this tool to respond to literature— think annotated timeline, character analysis, synopsis, book poster, or flyer. The only limit is the students' creativity.

Cost: Free/Pro option available $36/year
Must have written parental permission for students under the age of 13.

Explain Everything

https://explaineverything.com/

iPad app that allows you to annotate, animate, and narrate presentations and explanations. This is an excellent tool to use for digital storytelling, particularly with ESL populations.

- It can also be used to create lessons, tutorial, and how-to guides for the library and much more.

Cost: Varied options
Explain EverythingWhiteboard App: $15.99 one-time app purchase
Explain Everything: $2.67 per user/per year
*This option allows for real time collaboration
Explain Everything Classic: $7.99 one-time purchase

Kahoot

https://getkahoot.com/?utm_name=controller_app&utm_source=web_app&utm_medium=link

Kahoot is a free, online game-based platform that can be used for formative assessment.

- You can design your own learning game. Kahoot is excellent as a response to literature; try this instead of a traditional quiz or book report. Allow students to create their own Kahoot.
- Students do not have to join or provide personally identifiable information to play.

Cost: Free

Lino

http://en.linoit.com/

Use to post text, photos, and lists online.

- This can be used as a collaborative tool with groups of students or entire classes.

Cost: Free
Can be used with students of all ages.

Quizlet

https://quizlet.com/

Online flash cards. Students can use to learn unfamiliar words or as a vocabulary skill reinforcement.
- Students can respond to literature or interact with each other. Students can create their own cards or use ones already created.
- Best with middle school grades and above.

Cost: Free
$34.99 for expanded capabilities
Under 13 requires parental permission.

Powtoon

https://www.powtoon.com/

Online tools students use to create animations.

Cost: Free *Only records 45 seconds of video, medium quality
Classroom Basic $96/yr
Classroom Elite 192/yr
Edu Pro $59.88/yr

Padlet

https://padlet.com/

Online collaboration tool – teachers or librarians can pose questions about a literary work and students can all post their responses.

- Available in 29 languages including English, Spanish, French, Italian, and Portuguese.
- Users can upload pictures, videos, images, documents, music, and files.
- Available for iOs, Android, Kindle

Cost: Free; paid options available

Voki

http://www.voki.com/

Create custom avatars.

- Add voices to avatars.
- Post to a blog or website.
- Tool requires students to use a limited number of words, thus is excellent for getting students to summarize what they read. This can also be used to present a particular character's point of view.
- Great tool to use with ESL students as response to literature activities.

Cost: Free
$29.95 Classroom Subscription/yr

Kidblog

https://kidblog.org/home/

Blog site for students.
- Can be used with your book club, as a digital portfolio, or a space for creative writing.
- Provides a Google Apps for Education integration option.

Cost: $44/teacher librarian/yr
Users creating an account for students under the age of 13 must get written parental permission.

Book Creator

http://bookcreator.com/

App used to create books. Available for iPad, Android, and Windows.
- Students can create their own eBooks, including picture books, comic books, photo journals, cook books, and text books.

Cost: $4.99 one time purchase

Pic Collage

http://pic-collage.com/

Create collages with your photos, add stickers, texts, and other designs.
- Available for iOs, Android, and Windows.
- Students can upload their Pic Collage creation to See Saw. See Saw is mentioned in Chapter
- Students can use Pic Collage to create the Frayer Model Graphic organizer to learn vocabulary – includes the following elements:

- Definition (either from teacher or in student's own words)
- Examples
- Non-examples
- Characteristics or illustration of concept

Cost: Free; In-App purchases available

---

*These tools can be used to help not only ELL students practice using the English language but also to encourage all students to enhance their creativity and improve their communication and writing skills. The tools above also facilitate student creation and not just consumption. The tools make learning an active process for the students.

Incorporate Instructional Technology Tools To Empower ELL Students

Voice Thread

https://voicethread.com/

Students can create multimedia projects that integrate voice, image and text. The platform can be used for collaboration.

Cost: 1 educator – 50 students $79/year or $15/month

Simple English Wikipedia

https://simple.wikipedia.org/wiki/Main_Page

User contributed online encyclopedia for English Language Learners

Cost: Free

Google Translate

https://translate.google.com/

Google's free service instantly translates words, phrases, and web pages between English and over 100 other languages.

Cost: Free

These tools help students and parents practice using a new language.

Highlight Online Language Learning Tools

Duolingo

https://www.duolingo.com/

Language learning platform – learn Spanish, French, German, Italian, Portuguese plus 18 additional languages [more languages are in development].

Recommended for ages 13 and over
Cost: Free

Rosetta Stone

http://www.rosettastone.com

Rosetta Stone is a language learning solution. It is available as a download, stand-alone software or online. Rosetta Stone offers several solutions including products for purchase by individuals and K-12 solutions.

Cost: Individual $114/year
K – 12 solutions vary

Mango Languages

http://mangolanguages.com/index.html

Offers language learning for over 70 languages. Solutions are offered for individuals, as well as K – 12.

Cost: Free access available through some public libraries in the United States and Canada for individuals.

$20/month or $175/year individual access

K – 12 solution prices vary

These tools should not replace regular classroom instruction but could serve as additional support for ELL students. The tools offer students the opportunity to practice the language. Most are created for adults, so bear this in mind. This is also a good way to support parents of students whose first language may not be English.

Maximum Reader Engagement Activities

Here is a novel idea to promote reader engagement—not just among diverse readers, but all readers—try novel engineering. Novel engineering was developed at Tufts University as a component of STEM learning.[15] Students read literature, identify problems, and work to design solutions to the problems. Program designers state that novel engineering enhances reading curriculum, engages all learners, integrates different subjects, and builds skills such as communication, collaboration, and critical thinking.

Steps In The Novel Engineering Process

1. Read a book and identify problems –students find problems that the characters face.
2. Scope problems and brainstorm solutions –students work within the confines of the story as it is presented to come up with different solutions to the characters' problems.
3. Design a solution –students work together to build solutions to the problems.
4. Get feedback – students test their solutions and gather feedback.
5. Improve designs – Students use the information gathered to refine and perfect their solutions.
6. Share –students share their solutions with the class. This can be done through oral presentation, as a multimedia project, or in another innovative manner.

Source: http://www.novelengineering.org/

The Novel Engineering website presents several books with the design challenge already scoped out. You can use this as a guide and then develop projects based on books that reflect cultural diversity. One example presented is The Snowy Day by Ezra Jack Keats. The problem the student identified was that the character, Peter, wanted to keep a snow ball but it melted. The students designed portable snowball

---

[15] HINTON, M. 2017. Engineering Meets Kid Lit. *School Library Journal*, 63(1), 10-11.

savers as the solution. (http://www.novelengineering.org/)You can create your own design challenge for any book you select.

Book Chatters

If you want to get more students, teachers, and staff interested in reading more diverse titles, try *Book chatters*. *Book chatters* are more like informal presentations rather than book talks and are designed to pique the interests of young people. Students simply share about a book they really liked without giving away the ending. Kunzel and Hardesty described *book chatting* clubs as a way for student readers to talk about the books that interest them and allows students to demonstrate their enthusiasm for books they have been reading. It is suggested that *book chatting* be free-form.[161]

You can start a *book Chatters* Club by having students join while ensuring that a diverse group of students participate. Allow students to book chat about books that interest them. Undoubtedly, a group of diverse students will discuss books of diverse topics.

Book Club Mix Up

Create a book club that includes both students and adults. Allow students, parents, caregivers, and staff members to join your book club. Permit the students to give input as you develop your list of titles to read, but ensure that your reading list incorporates diverse selections.

Remember that families are diverse so the typical mother-daughter or father-son book club may not work. Many students are raised in single-parent households, by grandparents, or possibly in foster care. Sensitivity to different living arrangements may require you to have a book club mix up as opposed to a traditional family book club formats. Capitalize on technology and introduce a virtual component for your book club for parents and others who may be unable to attend a session in person due to work commitments. Allow these members to interact online. Participants can post video responses to discussion questions or share comments on a blog or site you create. Do remember to be CIPPA and COPA compliant. Make sure students posting to your webpage are over 13 and/or have written parental permission. Additionally, take care not to post personally identifiable information about students. For example, use a code instead of students' names.

---

[16] Kunzel, B. & Hardesty, C. (2006). *The Teen-Centered Book Club: Readers into Leaders*. Westport, Connecticut: Libraries Unlimited.

Set regular meeting days, such as the first Monday of every month. Meet in your library for an hour, serve affordable, healthy snacks if possible, and allow time for meaningful dialogue. A sample webpage outline is included below.
Make the experience exciting! Try to incorporate activities such as the ones that appear below.

- Ask parents or other adults to speak about their culture or experiences that may relate to a book you are reading.
- Invite authors to Skype with your club.
- Plan a field trip to a local museum or event that has a correlation to the book you are reading. [e.g., read *March* by John Lewis and visit the National Center for Civil and Human Rights in Atlanta, Georgia. https://www.civilandhumanrights.org
- If you can't afford to visit in person – plan a virtual field trip.
- Have dinner at a restaurant that serves cuisine from the country or culture read about in a book.
- Invite parents or students to bring in food that represents their culture.

Sample Book Discussion Questions/Activities for Print and eBooks

Reading A Print Book	Reading An Electronic Book
Place a sticky note on a passage that you liked or disliked.	Make a note electronically of passages that you liked or disliked.
Place a question mark sticky note on any passages, phrases, or sentences that did not make sense to you or that you didn't understand.	Make a note on a yellow sticky electronically of any passages, phrases, or sentences that did not make sense to you or that you didn't understand.
List any characters that made a lasting impression on you.	Highlight sections about a character that made a lasting impression on you.
Summarize the passage you read.	Summarize the passage you read.
List words you did not know on a sticky note or in a journal, then define the words.	Highlight in pink any words that you do not know. Use an online dictionary to record the meaning of the words.

Pop Up Library

Set up a "Pop Up Library" by using a book cart. A variation of the Pop Up library as discussed by Hauer is a *Diverse Pop Up Library*.[17] This cart of books would promote diversity both in school and possibly out of school. Books by diverse authors and about diversity would be placed on the cart. Consider placing books in the community where students live. Explore working in partnership with your local public library. Invite authors to speak at your Diverse *Pop Up Library* and partner with local restaurants or businesses to provide refreshments.

Birthday Books

Many schools celebrate students' birthdays. Often, students receive a small token or present for his or her birthday. Collect diverse books, via donations or other methods, and give these books to students as a birthday gift. You can have students become eligible to receive a birthday gift when they read a predetermined number of books. They can complete a reading log or take reading tests to prove they have actually met the reading goals.

It is also a great idea to present staff members with a birthday book. Remember to select diverse titles. If funding is a problem, seek donations from parents and local businesses, even authors in your school's community.

Speed Booking

Speed booking, think speed dating, allows you to feature books by diverse authors or books about diverse topics.

For a speed booking event, setup at least ten different books on a table or two. Have summary cards in front of each book or have pre-recorded information about each book available at a website. Set up a QR code for each website so that students can scan the code and go direly to the information about the book. Students can work independently or in pairs. Give each student 3 – 5 minutes with each book. After students have "dated" each book, allow them to make a final selection and check out the book of their choice.

---

[17] HAUER, B. (2016). Have Books, Will Travel. *School Library Journal*, 62(9), 16.

Family Read In

A family read in allows you to welcome all families to your school library. This can be targeted towards a specific grade level or done with the entire school. The read in allows children to share literature with their families. Create and customize your own celebration by sending home a welcome letter and having guest readers, which could be students' parents or other family members. Request that they share a book of personal cultural relevance. At your family read in, have students complete activities with their parents such as making their own bookmarks or recording podcasts. Additionally, students could challenge their family members to a game of chess, checkers, or other digital games.

An example promotion flyer appears on the next page. You can also create a SMORE for this purpose.

Read Around the World

Display a physical map on the library wall and have students place a pin or other item on a country each time a student reads or shares a book from a different country. Different classes can be represented by different color pins to encourage friendly competition. Give the class that reads books from the most countries a small prize.

Breakfast Buddies/Lunch Bunch/Dinner Den

Allow students to assemble in the library once per month, or at the frequency of your choosing, to share a meal and a book. Guide students towards selecting diverse books as topics of conversation. You can have your gathering before school, during lunch, or immediately after school. You can even take your group off site for a field trip to a local restaurant. Parental support and donations and business partnerships may provide you with the option of treating your students to a meal. Conversation over food can be quite enjoyable. Feature foods from various cultures at different intervals. If, for example, you are reading a book about the Civil Rights Era, invite a speaker or author to chat with students while dining. Bon appetite!

Character Interviews

Pair students and allow them to interview each other while they are in the role of characters from a book they have read. Take this a step further and use one of the technology tools presented in the chapter on tech tools. These interviews can be videotaped and/or audio recorded for sharing with the school and parents.

Dream Box

Students can create or decorate a box and then fill the box with their written dreams and hopes, or other inspirational messages. These hopes and dreams can be retained and then read aloud at the end of the school year. This is a great activity to complete at any time of the year or it can be done as a celebration of Rev. Dr. Martin Luther King Day.

Character Digital Scrapbook

Students can use electronic tools such as Linoit or Padlet to create a scrapbook of a character. Their electronic wall could contain items that represent the character. This could be physical attributes, likes and dislikes, as well as images that represent how the character thinks, feels, and acts.

Reading Cake Celebrate!

This is a great activity for Read Across America Day. You will need to begin this at least a month in advance.

- Have students vote on their favorite book. Allow students to make recommendations or just select your own list of books.
- Students can vote electronically using something like Google survey or with paper ballots.
- After the votes are tallied announce the winner and then have students design a cake that would represent the book selected.
- Take the students' design to your local bakery and have the cake made.
- Serve the cake to students on Read Across America Day.
- Bring in punch to add to the festive occasion.
- If you have a large student population you can invite students to participate who have checked out a predetermined amount of books.

Make sure to take plenty of pictures and share with your school and parents after the celebration has concluded.

Celebrity Readers

Invite a celebrity reader to come in and read to your students. This could be done on a special day, for example, during Hispanic Heritage Month, or on several days throughout the year. Invite speakers from diverse backgrounds and encourage them to read diverse books. Celebrity readers don't have to be mega wattage celebs—they could be your local city council member, school board member, religious leader, doctor, dentist, policeman, or nurse. Of course, professional athletes, singers, and movie stars make great readers too!

African American Read In

This is an excellent way to celebrate African American History Month. Visit the website, *www.ncte.org/aari*, for detailed information and a tool kit. Invite people to read works by African Americans. The African American Read In was established in 1990 by the Black Caucus of the National Council of Teachers of English to make literacy a significant part of Black History Month. *www.ncte.org/aari*

Writers Contest

What better way to grow diverse literature than to cultivate writers? Sponsor a contest that allows writers to share their work with the student population. You may elect to award a prize for the best writer. You could allow a panel to judge the writing or declare all entrants winners and publish all of the writing to your website or allow writers to share their works publically. You can hold a "book signing" of the winners and invite the school or certain grade levels to participate.

Tech Connect With Your Favorite Author = Skype/Google Hangout

Don't let geographical distance separate your students from their favorite author. Set up a Skype or Google hangout with authors to discuss their diverse work with the student body or with a particular class. You can extend this concept and Skype with scientists, engineers, or others in different countries. The sky is the limit. Let your creativity be your guide.

JOIN US FOR FAMILY READ IN

BRING YOUR FAVORITE BOOK TO READ WITH
YOUR CHILD & SHARE WITH A NEW FRIEND

FOOD

GAMES

PRIZES

ABC ELEMENTARY SCHOOL
MAY 2, 2019
SCHOOL LIBRARY

Sample Family Read-In Flyer

Promote Family Engagement Using Tech Tools

Communication is the foundation for any family engagement. Consistent, timely communication should be the bedrock of your approach to engaging families of diverse students. Earlier in the book, SMORE was explored. This is an excellent tool for communicating with families. You can use SMORE to share important events, activities, reading lists, and supportive parenting information.

Other Suggested Technology Tools To Enhance Family Engagement

https://www.remind.com/

Remind offers real time messages for your school, and messages can also be scheduled in advance. This tool helps you communicate efficiently. The cost is free. Ideas for using Remind:

- Communicate special events such as an African American History Book Fair or author visit for Hispanic Heritage Month
- Solicit volunteers
- Remind parents of opportunities to visit the library
- Text suggested diverse titles to read
- Text positive messages that affirm all cultures

Seesaw

http://web.seesaw.me/

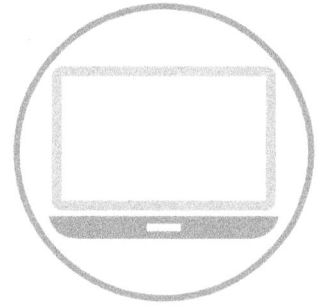

Seesaw is a student-driven digital portfolio and parent communication tool. Librarians could use Seesaw to document projects done in the school library, such as book talks on diverse titles. These activities can be shared online with parents. You can have students upload texts, photos, videos, drawings, and weblinks. Seesaw also offers a blog feature. Students can blog easily and connect what they are reading and writing to the global community. Seesaw is available for free. Seesaw Plus costs $120 per teacher. SeeSaw is targeted for use with K – 5 students.

> *"We are of course a nation of differences.*
> *Those differences don't make us weak.*
> *They're the source of our strength."*
>
> *Jimmy Carter*

Useful Links

https://www.leeandlow.com/
Lee and Low Publishers

https://www.docsteach.org/
Online tool for teaching with primary source documents, National Archives

http://www.enchantedlearning.com/
Online educational material for grades K – 12 on a wide range of topics

http://glbtrt.ala.org/rainbowbooks/rainbow-books-lists
Book List for GLBT Book Month

http://teacher.scholastic.com/activities/bhistory/underground_railroad/
Interactive Underground Railroad

http://www.thekingcenter.org/about-dr-king
Information about Rev. Dr. Martin Luther King, Jr.

http://kids.nationalgeographic.com/explore/history/martin-luther-king-jr/
Martin Luther King, Jr. Information

https://www.nps.gov/malu/index.htm
National Parks Service – King birthplace

https://www.docsteach.org/documents/document/exhibit-1-in-city-of-memphis-vs-martin-luther-king
Flyer – Sanitation Workers in Memphis 1968 – March for Justice and Jobs (Dr. King)

http://www.tolerance.org/
Various resources that support equity founded by the Southern Poverty Law Center, includes classroom resources, professional development, magazines, and much more

http://www.loc.gov/exhibits/african/intro.html
The African-American Mosaic
A Library of Congress Resource Guide for the Study of Black History and Culture

http://www.history.com/topics/black-history/black-history-month
History Channel – African American History Month

http://digital.nypl.org/schomburg/images_aa19/
Images of African Americans from the 19th Century

https://nmaahc.si.edu/
National Museum of African American History and Culture

https://www.smore.com/educators
SMORE

Diverse Collection & Programming Smart Goals

Smart Goal – Collection

BY _____(DATE) INCREASE THE NUMBER OF DIVERSE TITLES BY ____%.

BY _____ (DATE) INCREASE THE NUMBER OF DIVERSE TITLES IN THE _____
SECTION (FICTION/NONFICTION/BIOGRAPHY) BY ____%.

Smart Goal – Programming

BY _____ (DATE) FACILITATE _____ (#)PROGRAMS SPECIFICALLY TARGETED TO
CULTIVATE DIVERSITY IN THE SCHOOL LIBRARY PROGRAM.
LIST PROGRAMS:

EX. AUTHOR SKYPE VISIT, NOVEL ENGINEERING OF A DIVERSE TITLE

_____

_____

Smart Goal – Parental Involvement

BY _____ (DATE) FACILITATE _____ (#) PROGRAMS/ACTIVITIES SPECIFICALLY TARGETED
TO ENGAGE PARENTS IN THE SCHOOL LIBRARY PROGRAM.
LIST PROGRAMS OR ACTIVITIES:

LIST PROGRAMS OR ACTIVITIES:

_____

_____

Keep Calm and Carry On

Welcoming the world into your school library program will undoubtedly bring to the surface fears and feelings of confusion to some in your school. Don't be surprised, and by all means don't stop what you are doing. As a librarian you are no stranger to controversy. Diverse materials may make some uncomfortable and defensive. Just be prepared if you find things to be a bit shaky. Realize all of the students and staff in your building are counting on you to provide them with opportunities to access information, all types of information.

Here are five tips for keeping calm and carrying on.

1. Respond to hate and fear with continuous calm courage.
2. Don't try to change others' opinions on controversial issues—just present information.
3. Always be respectful.
4. If books or property are defaced in protest, immediately involve your school's administration, district personnel, and law enforcement (as appropriate).
5. Lean on other library professionals for support.

*Remember your work makes a difference!

Index

About the Author

Michelle Easley is an expert in all things school library. She is a national presenter and published author. She is published in *Teacher Librarian* and the American Association's *Knowledge Quest*. She has served as a teacher and school library media specialist at all levels, elementary, middle and high school. Michelle coordinated media programs for schools on all military bases – Air Force, Army, Marines, Coast Guard and Navy, in the United States, Cuba and Puerto Rico for the Domestic Dependent Elementary and Secondary Schools operated by the Department of Defense Education Activity. She serves in a leadership capacity for a public school system in Atlanta, Georgia. She is currently the president of the Georgia Library Media Association.

Michelle received both a Bachelor of Science degree and a Master of Business Administration degree from Florida A&M University, a Master of Arts and Teaching degree from Emory University, and the Specialist in Education degree from Georgia State University. She resides in Atlanta.

Thank you for buying this book published by

Positive Push Press, LLC.
www.positivepushpresss.com

To receive special offers, bonus content, and news about our latest publications, sign up for our newsletters.

The author is available for speaking engagements as a keynote speaker, workshop or conference facilitator, professional development leader, or upon your request. Additionally, the author can provide customized consulting services. Please contact Positive Push Press, LLC for additional information.

To purchase multiple copies of this book at a discounted rate contact us. For permission to reprint any portion of this book please contact our permissions department.

Visit us at
www.michelleeasley.com

www.ingramcontent.com/pod-product-compliance
Lightning Source LLC
La Vergne TN
LVHW081317060426
835509LV00015B/1561